Eid Mi

to Nick ... ...

Lots Love Mum xxx

بسم الله الرحمن الرحيم

المحجة

في سير الدلجة

شرح حديث

«لن ينجي أحدًا منكم عمله»

al-Ḥāfiẓ ibn Rajab al-Ḥanbalī

The JOURNEY to ALLĀH

An explanation to the Ḥadīth,

"Your actions alone will not save any of you"

being a translation of his *al-Maḥajjah fī Sayri'l-Dulja*

دار السنة

AN EXPLANATION TO THE ḤADĪTH,

"Your actions alone will not save any of you"

[BUKHĀRĪ #6463]

THE JOURNEY TO ALLĀH

An Explanation to the Ḥadīth,

"Your actions alone will not save any of you"

Translated from the original Arabic by
Abū Rumaysah

دار السنة

DĀR AS-SUNNAH PUBLISHERS

BIRMINGHAM

Second Edition Published in Great Britain, August 2012 / Ramaḍān 1433H
by Dār as-Sunnah Publishers

DĀR AS-SUNNAH PUBLISHERS
P.O. Box 9818, Birmingham, B11 4WA, United Kingdom

W: www.darassunnah.com
E: info@darassunnah.com
E: daar-us-sunnah@mail.com

British Library Cataloguing in publication Data.
A catalogue record for this book is available from the British Library.

Title: The Journey to Allāh
by: al-Ḥāfiẓ ibn Rajab al-Ḥanbalī (d.795H)
Translated from the original Arabic by Abū Rumaysah

ISBN 1-904336-17-5
Paper-back

First Edition 1428AH/2007CE
Second Edition 1433AH/2012
Typeset by: Dār as-Sunnah Publishers

CONTENT

THE AUTHOR

Ḥāfiẓ Abū'l-Faraj ibn Rajab al-Ḥanbalī

He is the Imām and Ḥāfiẓ, Zaynu'l-Dīn 'Abdu'l-Raḥmān ibn Aḥmad ibn 'Abdu'l-Raḥmān ibn al-Ḥasan ibn Muḥammad ibn Abū'l-Barakāt Mas'ūd al-Sulamī al-Ḥanbalī al-Dimashqī. His agnomen was Abū'l-Faraj, and his nickname was Ibn Rajab, which was the nickname of his grandfather who was born in that month.

He was born in Baghdād in 736H and was raised by a knowledgeable and pious family. He died on a Monday night, the fourth of Ramaḍān, 795H in al-Ḥumariyyah, Damascus.

He learned and took knowledge from the greatest scholars of his time. In Damascus, he studied under Ibn Qayyim al-Jawziyyah, Zaynu'l-Dīn al-'Irāqī, ibn an-Naqīb, Muḥammad ibn Ismā'īl al-Khabbāz, Dāwūd ibn Ibrāhīm al-'Aṭṭār, ibn Qāṭī al-Jabal and Aḥmad ibn 'Abdu'l-Hādī al-Ḥanbalī. In Makkah, he heard from al-Fakhr 'Uthmān ibn Yūsuf al-Nuwayrī. In Jerusalem, he heard from al-Ḥāfiẓ al-'Alā'ī. In Egypt, he heard from Ṣadru'l-Dīn Abū'l-Fatḥ al-Maydūmī and Nāṣiru'l-Dīn ibn al-Mulūk.

Many students of knowledge came to him to study under him. Amongst the most famous of his students were: Abū'l-'Abbās

Aḥmad ibn Abū Bakr ibn 'Alī al-Ḥanbalī; Abū'l-Faḍl Aḥmad ibn Naṣr ibn Aḥmad; Dāwūd ibn Sulaymān al-Mawsilī; 'Abdu'l-Raḥmān ibn Aḥmad ibn Muḥammad al-Muqrī'; Zaynū'l-Dīn 'Abdu'l-Raḥmān ibn Sulaymān ibn Abū'l-Karam; Abū Dharr al-Zarkashī; al-Qāḍī 'Alā'ū'l-Dīn ibn al-Lahām al-Ba'lī; and Aḥmad ibn Ṣayfū'l-Dīn al-Ḥamawī.

Ibn Rajab devoted himself to knowledge and spent the vast majority of his time researching, writing, authoring, teaching, and giving legal rulings.

Many scholars praised him for his vast knowledge, asceticism and expertise in the Ḥanbalī school of thought. Ibn Qāḍī Shuhbah said of him, 'He read and became proficient in the various fields of science. He engrossed himself with the issues of the madhhab until he mastered it. He devoted himself to the occupation of knowledge of the texts, defects and meanings of the ḥadīth.'[1]

Ibn Ḥajr said of him, 'He was highly proficient in the science of ḥadīth in terms of the names of reporters, their biographies, their paths of narration and awareness of their meanings.'[2]

Ibn Mufliḥ said of him, 'He is the Shaykh, the great scholar, the Ḥāfiẓ, the ascetic, the Shaykh of the Ḥanbalī madhhab and he authored many beneficial works.'[3]

He wrote many beneficial works, some of them outstanding

[1] Ibn Qāḍī al-Shuhbah, *Tārīkh*, vol. 3, p. 195.

[2] ibn Ḥajr, *Inbā'u'l-Ghamr*, vol. 1, p. 460.

[3] *al-Maqṣad al-Arshad*, vol. 2, p. 81.

such as *al-Qawā'id al-Kubrā fi'l-Furū'* about which it was said, 'It is one of the wonders of this age.'[4] His commentary to al-Tirmidhī is said to be the most extensive and best ever written so much so that al-'Irāqī; about whom ibn Ḥajr said, 'He was the wonder of his age'; would ask for his help when compiling his own commentary to the same book.

- Moreover he has many valuable monographs explaining various aḥādīth such as: *Sharḥ Ḥadīth Mā Dhi'bāni Jāi'ān Ursilā fi Ghanam*; *Ikhtiyār al-Awlā Sharḥ Ḥadīth Ikhtiṣām al-Mala' al-A'lā*; *Nūr al-Iqtibās fi Sharḥ Waṣiyyah al-Nabī li ibn 'Abbās*; and *Kashfu'l-Kurbah fi Wasfi Ḥāli Ahli-l-Ghurbah.*

- In exegesis his works include: *Tafsīr Sūrah al-Ikhlāṣ*; *Tafsīr Sūrah al-Fātiḥah*; *Tafsīr Sūrah al-Naṣr*; and *al-Istighnā' bi'l-Qur'ān.*

- In ḥadīth his works include: *Sharḥ 'Ilal al-Tirmidhī*; *Fatḥu'l-Bārī Sharḥ Ṣaḥīḥ al-Bukhārī*; and *Jāmi' al-'Ulūm wa'l-Ḥikam.*

- In fiqh his works include: *al-Istikhrāj fi Aḥkām al-Kharāj*; and *al-Qawā'id al-Fiqhiyyah.*

- In biographies his works include the monumental *Dhayl 'alā Ṭabaqāti'l-Ḥanābilah.*

- In exhortation his works include: *Laṭā'if al-Ma'ārif* and *al-Takhwīf min al-Nār.*

[4] ibn 'Abdu'l-Hādī, *Dhayl 'alā Ṭabaqāt ibn Rajab,* p. 38.

INTRODUCTION

With the Name of Allāh, the All-Merciful, the Most Merciful

Bukhārī records on the authority of Abū Hurayrah (*raḍiyAllāhu 'anhu*) that the Prophet (ﷺ) said, "Your actions alone will not save any of you." They asked, 'Messenger of Allāh, not even you?' He replied, "Not even me, unless Allāh were to envelop me in His mercy. Be firm; steadfast and balanced; and journey [to Allāh] in the beginning of the day, the end of the day, and a portion of the latter part of the night. Moderation, moderation! Through this will you attain your goal!"[5]

He also recorded this ḥadīth in another place with the wording, "This religion is easy, none makes it hard upon himself except that it overwhelms him; therefore be firm, steadfast, and balanced; upon which have glad tidings! Seek help in this by journeying [to Allāh] at the beginning of the day, at the end of the day, and a portion of the latter part of the night."[6]

---

[5] Bukhārī #6463.

[6] Ibid. #39.

He also records on the authority of 'Ā'ishah (*radiyAllāhu 'anhā*) that the Prophet (ﷺ) said, "Be firm, steadfast, and balanced upon which have glad tidings for indeed actions alone will not cause one to enter Paradise." They asked, 'Messenger of Allāh, not even you?' He replied, "Not even me, unless Allāh were to envelop me in His forgiveness and mercy."[7]

He also records on her authority that the Prophet (ﷺ) said, "Be firm, steadfast, and balanced: know that your actions alone will not be a cause for your entry into Paradise and that the most beloved actions to Allāh are those that are done continuously and persistently, even if they be few."[8]

These noble aḥādīth[9] detail a great and important principle from which stem many issues related to the journey to Allāh while wayfaring along His Path.

---

[7] Ibid. #6467.

[8] Ibid. #6464.

[9] Muslim #2816-7113 records the ḥadīth of Abū Hurayrah that the Prophet (ﷺ) said, "There is not a single person whose deeds will enter him into Paradise." It was asked, 'Messenger of Allāh, not even you?' He replied, "Not even me, unless Allāh were to envelop me in His mercy."

He also records #2816-7121 on the authority of Jābir that he heard the Messenger of Allāh (ﷺ) saying, "The deeds of any one of you will not enter him into Paradise or save him from the Fire, not even me unless it be through the mercy of Allāh."

The ḥadīth is also recorded on the authority of Abū Sa'īd by Aḥmad #11486; Abū Mūsā, Usāmah ibn Sharīk, Sharīk ibn Ṭāriq, and Asad ibn Kurz by Ṭabarānī, *al-Kabīr* #493-1001-6549-7218-7221.

CHAPTER ONE

The Great Principle

As for the principle, it is that the deeds of man are not sufficient to deliver him from Hellfire, or to grant him entry into Paradise; instead this can only come about through the mercy of Allāh and His forgiveness. The Qur'ān supports this meaning in many places such as His sayings,

فَٱلَّذِينَ هَاجَرُوا۟ وَأُخْرِجُوا۟
مِن دِيَٰرِهِمْ وَأُوذُوا۟ فِى سَبِيلِى وَقَٰتَلُوا۟ وَقُتِلُوا۟ لَأُكَفِّرَنَّ
عَنْهُمْ سَيِّـَٔاتِهِمْ وَلَأُدْخِلَنَّهُمْ جَنَّٰتٍ تَجْرِى مِن تَحْتِهَا
ٱلْأَنْهَٰرُ ثَوَابًا مِّنْ عِندِ ٱللَّهِ ۗ وَٱللَّهُ عِندَهُۥ حُسْنُ ٱلثَّوَابِ ﴿١٩٥﴾

Those who migrated and were driven from their homes and suffered harm in My way and fought and were killed, I will erase their bad actions from them and admit them into Gardens with rivers flowing beneath them as a reward from Allāh[10]

يُبَشِّرُهُمْ رَبُّهُم بِرَحْمَةٍ مِّنْهُ وَرِضْوَٰنٍ وَجَنَّٰتٍ لَّهُمْ فِيهَا
نَعِيمٌ مُّقِيمٌ ﴿٢١﴾

[10] *Āli 'Imrān* (3): 195

Their Lord gives them the good news of his mercy and good pleasure and Gardens where they will enjoy everlasting delight, remaining in them timelessly, for ever and ever[11]

تُؤْمِنُونَ بِٱللَّهِ وَرَسُولِهِۦ وَتُجَٰهِدُونَ
فِى سَبِيلِ ٱللَّهِ بِأَمْوَٰلِكُمْ وَأَنفُسِكُمْ ۚ ذَٰلِكُمْ خَيْرٌ لَّكُمْ إِن كُنتُمْ تَعْلَمُونَ ﴿١١﴾
يَغْفِرْ لَكُمْ ذُنُوبَكُمْ وَيُدْخِلْكُمْ جَنَّٰتٍ تَجْرِى مِن تَحْتِهَا ٱلْأَنْهَٰرُ

...it is to believe in Allāh and His Messenger and to do Jihād in the Way of Allāh with your wealth and your selves. That is better for you if you only knew. He will forgive you your wrong actions and admit you into Gardens with rivers flowing beneath them...[12]

mentioning victory and entry into Paradise alongside forgiveness and mercy thereby proving that this cannot be attained except by these.

Some of the Salaf said, 'The Hereafter consists either of Allāh's forgiveness or the Fire; and this world is either a source of Allāh's protection or a source of destruction.' On his deathbed, Muḥammad ibn Wāsiʿ bid farewell to his companions saying, 'Peace be upon you, either to the Fire or to the forgiveness of Allāh.'[13]

---

[11] *al-Tawbah* (9): 22

[12] *al-Ṣaff* (61): 11-12

[13] Abū Nuʿaym, *al-Ḥilyah*, vol. 2, p. 348 #199.

As for the saying of Allāh,

وَتِلْكَ ٱلْجَنَّةُ ٱلَّتِىٓ أُورِثْتُمُوهَا بِمَا كُنتُمْ تَعْمَلُونَ ﴿٧٢﴾

That is the Garden you will be made to inherit for what you did.[14]

كُلُوا۟ وَٱشْرَبُوا۟ هَنِيٓـًٔۢا بِمَآ أَسْلَفْتُمْ فِى ٱلْأَيَّامِ ٱلْخَالِيَةِ ﴿٢٤﴾

...eat and drink with relish for what you did before in days gone by![15]

the scholars differed concerning the meaning of this, falling into two opinions:

1) Entry into Paradise is accorded by His mercy, but the assignment of ranking and station in Paradise is done in accordance to the deeds one performed.[16] ibn 'Uyaynah said, 'They were of the opinion that salvation from the Fire occurs through the forgiveness of Allāh, entry into Paradise occurs by His grace, and the apportioning of ranking occurs in accordance to one's deeds.'

2) That the *ba* which has been mentioned in His sayings, ***"for what you did", "for what you did before in days gone by"*** is the *ba* used to indicate causality (*sabab*). Hence the meaning is that Allāh has appointed deeds to be the means for entry into Paradise. The *ba* which has been negated in his (ﷺ) saying, "Actions

[14] *al-Zukhruf* (43): 72

[15] *al-Ḥāqqah* (69): 24

[16] Ibn Ḥajr, *Fatḥ al-Bārī*, vol. 11, p. 295, quoted this opinion from ibn Baṭṭāl.

alone will not cause one to enter Paradise" is the *ba* indicating comparison and compensation (*muqābalah*) and replacing like for like (*mu'āwidah*).[17] The meaning of the ḥadīth would then be that none deserves entry into Paradise by virtue of the deeds he has performed. Through this explanation the erroneous understanding that Paradise is the imbursement of deeds is dispelled: the understanding that the person, by virtue of his deeds alone, has the right to be granted entry into Paradise by Allāh; just as one who pays the price for a commodity has the right that it be given him by the seller. This explanation makes clear that actual entry comes to pass by the grace and mercy of Allāh, and that deeds are a cause for the entry into Paradise.

Therefore actual entry into Paradise is dependant upon the grace of Allāh, His forgiveness and mercy: He is the one who blessed the person with the means and the result of that means. Hence entry is not a direct outcome of actions in and of themselves. It is recorded in the Ṣaḥīḥ that the Prophet (ﷺ) said, "Allāh, Blessed and Exalted, said to Paradise: You are My mercy, I show mercy through you to whoever I will of My servants."

The servants have no right over Him that He must render,
Never! Neither, in His presence, is any effort wretched.
If they are punished, then by His Justice; if they are in bliss,
Then by His beneficence. He is the Kind, the Vast.

[17] Ibid., quoting this opinion from Kirmānī.
Meaning like a business transaction in which one buys a commodity and gives, in return, its equivalent price.

1.1 *al-Ḥamdulillāh* is the Imbursement of Every Favour

If it is said: but Ḥabīb ibn al-Shahīd reports al-Ḥasan as saying, '*al-Ḥamdulillāh*[18] is the imbursement of every favour and *Lā ilāha illAllāh*[19] is the imbursement for Paradise.'

The meaning of this statement has also been reported from the Prophet (ﷺ) on the authority of Anas, Abū Dharr and others. Even though the isnāds of all these aḥādīth contain weakness,[20] the meaning is supported by the saying of Allāh,

﴿إِنَّ ٱللَّهَ ٱشْتَرَىٰ مِنَ ٱلْمُؤْمِنِينَ أَنفُسَهُمْ وَأَمْوَٰلَهُم
بِأَنَّ لَهُمُ ٱلْجَنَّةَ ۚ يُقَٰتِلُونَ فِى سَبِيلِ ٱللَّهِ فَيَقْتُلُونَ
وَيُقْتَلُونَ ۖ وَعْدًا عَلَيْهِ حَقًّا فِى ٱلتَّوْرَىٰةِ وَٱلْإِنجِيلِ
وَٱلْقُرْءَانِ ۚ وَمَنْ أَوْفَىٰ بِعَهْدِهِۦ مِنَ ٱللَّهِ ۚ فَٱسْتَبْشِرُوا۟
بِبَيْعِكُمُ ٱلَّذِى بَايَعْتُم بِهِۦ ۚ وَذَٰلِكَ هُوَ ٱلْفَوْزُ ٱلْعَظِيمُ ﴿١١١﴾

Allāh has bought from the believers their selves and their wealth in return for the Garden: they fight in the Way of Allāh and they kill and are killed. It is a promise binding on Him in the Torah, the Injīl and the Qur'ān and who is truer to his contract than Allāh? Rejoice then in the bar-

[18] Tr: All praise is due to Allāh.

[19] Tr: There is none worthy of worship save Allāh.

[20] Ghazālī quoted them in *Iḥyā' 'Ulūm al-Dīn*, vol. 1, p. 299, and 'Irāqī said, 'Recorded by ibn 'Adī and Mustaghfirī and none of them are authentic.'

> **gain you have made. That is the supreme triumph.**[21]

Here, Paradise has been appointed the imbursement for self and property.

The response to this is that Allāh, Glorious and Exalted is He; through His beneficence, mercy, kindness, and generosity; has addressed His servants in a way that would encourage them to obey Him, using language and concepts that they can readily understand and relate to. He placed Himself in the position of a buyer and debtor, and placed them in the position of sellers and creditors. This then encourages them to answer His call and rush to His obedience. In reality, however, everything belongs to Him and is granted by His grace and mercy: the self and property belong to Him and this is why He commanded us to say at the onset of calamity,

إِنَّا لِلَّهِ وَإِنَّآ إِلَيْهِ رَٰجِعُونَ

> **To Allāh we belong and to Him are we returning.**[22]

Despite this, He commends those who expend their selves and properties for His sake, comparing them to sellers and creditors. Therefore man is likened to someone who has property which he can sell and give as a loan to someone else who does not possess it.

In the same way, all deeds come about as a result of His grace

[21] *al-Tawbah* (9): 111

[22] *al-Baqarah* (2): 156

and mercy, yet He commends those who perform them, attributes the deeds to them, and appoints them to be a show of gratitude, and return, for His favours.

1.2 Elucidation of the meaning of 'favours'

Ibn Mājah records on the authority of Anas that the Prophet (ﷺ) said, "There is no favour which Allāh bestows upon His servant for which he says, '*al-Ḥamdulillāh,*' except that which he gave was better than that which he took."[23] This was also stated by 'Umar ibn 'Abdu'l-'Azīz,[24] al-Ḥasan,[25] and others from amongst the Salaf.[26]

The meaning of this has troubled a great number of scholars, past and present, but if it is understood in the light of our preceding discussion, its meaning is obvious. The meaning of favour mentioned in the ḥadīth is worldly favour and the statement of praising Allāh is one of the religious favours. Religious favours are better than worldly favours. Now, because the favour of praising Allāh has been attributed to the servant since he articulated it, Allāh considers him as giving the greater favour as a

[23] Recorded by ibn Mājah #3805 on the authority of Anas.

Būḍayrī said, 'Its isnād is ḥasan,' as did Suyūṭī, *al-Durr al-Manthūr*, vol. 1, p. 34, and Albānī, *Ṣaḥīḥ al-Targhīb* #1573 ruled it ḥasan.

What "he gave," was the statement of praise and what "he took," was the favour. Refer to Sindī, *Ḥāshiyah 'alā Ibn Mājah,* vol. 4, pg. 251.

[24] Bayhaqī, *Shu'ab al-Īmān* #10038.

[25] Ibid. #4406 and Ibn Abī al-Dunya, *al-Shukr* #111.

[26] Such as Bakr ibn 'Abdullāh, ibid. #4408.

return for the original favour.[27] This is why it is mentioned in a narration, '*al-Ḥamdulillāh*, with a praise that befits and suffices His favours; represses His retribution; and acts as return for His addition.'[28]

When understood in this light, the statement of praise is the imbursement of Paradise.

1.3 Both Paradise & Deeds are from the Grace of Allāh

Therefore, to be correct, both Paradise and deeds are granted to the believing servants by the grace and mercy of Allāh. This is why the inhabitants of Paradise will say upon entering it,

ٱلْحَمْدُ لِلَّهِ ٱلَّذِى هَدَىٰنَا لِهَٰذَا
وَمَا كُنَّا لِنَهْتَدِىَ لَوْلَآ أَنْ هَدَىٰنَا ٱللَّهُ لَقَدْ جَآءَتْ رُسُلُ رَبِّنَا بِٱلْحَقِّ

Praise be to Allāh who guided us to this! We would not have been guided had Allāh not guided us. Verily the Messengers of our Lord came with the Truth.[29]

[27] When in reality it is Allāh who granted both.

[28] Ibn Ḥajr, *Talkhīṣ al-Ḥabīr*, vol. 4, p. 171, said, 'It is reported that Jibrīl taught Ādam these words, 'al-Ḥamdulillāh, with a praising that befits, and suffices, His favours and recompenses His addition,' and then said, 'I have taught you comprehensive words of praise.' Ibn al-Ṣalāḥ said in his discussion to *al-Wasīṭ*, 'Ḍaʿīf isnād, munqaṭī.' Nawawī, *al-Rawḍah*, said, 'I found it in ibn al-Ṣalāḥ, *al-Amālī*... and it is muʿḍal.'

[29] *al-Aʿrāf (7)*: 43

After they acknowledge that it was through the favour of Allāh that they were granted Paradise, and that it was through His favour that they were they granted the accord to enact the means leading to it, i.e. His guidance, and after having praised Him for this, they are rewarded with the call,

أَن تِلْكُمُ ٱلْجَنَّةُ أُورِثْتُمُوهَا بِمَا كُنتُمْ تَعْمَلُونَ ﴿٤٣﴾

Behold! This is the Garden you will be made to inherit for what you did.[30]

Their deeds were attributed to them and they were shown appreciation for them.

It is with this overall meaning that some of the Salaf said, 'When a servant commits a sin and says, "My Lord, You decreed this for me!" His Lord will say, "You are the one who sinned and disobeyed Me!" Now if the servant says, "My Lord, I erred, committed a sin, and wrought evil," Allāh will respond by saying, "I decreed this upon you and I will forgive you."'

1.4 Misery and Felicity occur Through His Justice and Mercy

The true purport of his (ﷺ) words, "Your actions alone will not save any of you", "Actions alone will not cause one to enter Paradise" can be be further understood when it is realised that the reward of good deeds, multiplied manifold, only comes about by the beneficence and grace of Allāh, Mighty and Magnificent. He recompenses a good deed tenfold to seven-hundred fold to

[30] *al-A'rāf* (7): 43

whatever He wills.[31] Were He to recompense a good deed with its like, in the same way that He does for an evil deed, good deeds would never have the strength to render void the evil deeds, and one would surely be destroyed.

Ibn Mas'ūd (*raḍiyAllāhu 'anhu*) said, while describing good deeds, 'If one is an ally (*walī*) of Allāh, and there remain an atoms weight of good [after the mutual recompense], Allāh would increase this manifold such that he enter Paradise through it.[32] If he be one for whom misery is decreed, the Angel says, "My Lord, His good deeds have vanished yet many more people remain seeking [mutual recompense]." He will reply, "Take their evil deeds and add them to his evil deeds, then prepare for him a place of torment in the Fire!"'[33]

Therefore it becomes clear that Allāh multiplies the good deeds of those He wishes felicity for until they are able to pay off any penalties [from any who seek mutual recompense]; and if, after all this, there remains even an atoms weight worth of good, Allāh will multiply this until He enters Paradise through it. All this by His grace and beneficence! However, whoever Allāh has decreed misery for; his deeds will not be multiplied to the extent that they are able to pay off his penalties. Instead any good deeds performed by this latter person will only be multiplied ten-fold,

---

[31] Muslim #131/338.

[32] This meaning is also recorded by Ḥākim #7641, 7642 on the authority of ibn 'Abbās that the Prophet (ﷺ) said, "....then if a good deed remains, Allāh will expand generously [a place] for him in Paradise."
Ḥākim said it was ṣaḥīḥ with Dhahabī agreeing.

[33] Abū Nu'aym, vol. 4, p. 224 #5328; ibn al-Mubārak, *al-Zuhd* #1416.

apportioned amongst his creditors who will accept them all and yet still require further repayment for remaining injustices, and therefore their bad deeds are piled onto his, thereby causing him to enter the Fire. This by His justice![34]

It is in this light that Yaḥyā ibn Muʿādh said, 'When He extends His grace, not a single evil deed remains for that person! When His justice is brought forth, not a single good deed remains for that person.'[35]

It is also established in Bukhārī and Muslim that the Prophet (ﷺ) said, "Whoever's account is scrutinised will be destroyed",[36]

---

[34] Muslim #2581/6579 records on the authority of Abū Hurayrah that the Messenger of Allāh (ﷺ) asked, "Do you know the bankrupt person is?" They said, 'A bankrupt man amongst us is one who has neither dirham with him nor wealth.' He said, "The bankrupt person of my nation would be he who comes on the Day of Resurrection with prayers and fasts and Zakāt but he hurled abuses upon this person, brought calumny against that person, unlawfully consumed the wealth of that person, shed the blood of that person, and beat that person. So his good deeds would be credited to the deeds of those people [by way of retaliation] and if his good deeds fall short to clear the account, their sins would be added to his and he would be thrown in the Fire."

Muslim #2582/6580 records on the authority of Abū Hurayrah that the Messenger of Allāh (ﷺ) said, "All rights will be restored to their owners on the Day of Judgment. Even a hornless goat that is butted by a ram will have justice."

[35] Abū Nuʿaym, vol. 10, p. 69 #14593.

[36] Bukhārī #6537 and Muslim #2876/7227, 7228 on the authority 'Ā'ishah. The wording of Bukhārī has 'Ā'ishah then asking, 'Does not Allāh say, ***"Then he who is given his Record in his right hand, soon will his account be taken by an easy reckoning,"*** [*al-Inshiqāq* (84): 7-8]?' He replied, "That is not the scrutiny that is a presentation, whoever's account is scrutinised will be punished."

in another narration, "...will be punished"[37] and in another narration, "...will be defeated."[38]

Abū Nuʿaym records on the authority of ʿAlī that the Prophet (ﷺ) said, "Allāh revealed to a Prophet amongst the Prophets of the Children of Israel, 'Say to those who obey Me amongst your nation that they should not overly rely on their deeds for on the Day of Judgment I will not settle the accounts of a servant I wish to punish except that I will punish him. Say to those who disobey me amongst your nation that they should not despair for I readily forgive even the great sins'"[39]

ʿAbdu'l-ʿAzīz ibn Abū Rawwād said, 'Allāh inspired Dāwūd (*ʿalayhis-salām*) saying, "Dāwūd, give glad tidings to the sinners and warn those who give in charity." Surprised, Dāwūd said, "My Lord, why should I give glad tidings to the sinners and warn those who give in charity?" He replied, "Give glad tidings to the sinners that there is no sin that I find too grievous to forgive[40] and warn those who give in charity that there is no servant upon

---

[37] Bukhārī #6536 and Muslim #2876/7225 on the authority ʿĀ'ishah.
This wording mentioned above is also recorded by Tirmidhī #3338 on the authority of Anas.

[38] Ḥākim #8728 and Dhahabī said the isnād contained a weak narrator.
Ibn Abī Shaybah, vol. 13, p. 360, has the wording, "...will not be forgiven," and ibn al-Mubārak, *al-Zuhd* #1324 also records this wording as a statement of ʿĀ'ishah.

[39] Ṭabarānī, *al-Awsaṭ* #4844.
Its isnād contains a weak narrator as per Haythamī, vol. 1, p. 307. The author, *Jāmiʿ al-ʿUlūm*, vol. 1, p. 177, said the isnād was ḍaʿīf.

[40] Even *shirk* if one repents from it.

whom I mete My justice and judgment except that he is destroyed.'"[41]

Ibn 'Uyaynah said, 'Scrutiny here means to undergo the evil of a thorough examination such that nothing is leftover.'[42]

Ibn Yazīd said, 'The severe reckoning is that which contains no pardoning[43] and the easy reckoning is that in which ones sins are forgiven and good deeds accepted.'[44]

All of these narrations show that that servant cannot possibly succeed without forgiveness, mercy and the overlooking of his faults. They also show that when Allāh enacts pure justice upon the servant, he will certainly be destroyed.

---

[41] Abū Nu'aym, vol. 8, p. 211 #11906.

[42] Ibn Abī Shaybah #35644 records that Abū al-Jawzā' said concerning the verse, ***"...and dread a woeful reckoning."*** [*al-Ra'd* (13): 21], 'It means to undergo a questioning about one's deeds.'

[43] Ar: *'Afw*: the overlooking of a sin.

[44] Ṭabarī #34361, 36738

Aḥmad #24215-25515 records on the authority of 'Ā'ishah that she asked the Messenger of Allāh (ﷺ) what the ***"easy reckoning"*** [*al-Inshiqāq* (84):8] was to which he replied, "A person has his sins presented before him only to have them overlooked. For sure, the one whose account is questioned will be destroyed."

It was declared ṣaḥīḥ by ibn Ḥibbān #7372, ibn Khuzaymah #849, and Ḥākim #936 with Dhahabī agreeing.

1.5 Allāh's Blessings can Never be Truly Repaid

This is further clarified by His saying,

ثُمَّ لَتُسْـَٔلُنَّ يَوْمَئِذٍ عَنِ ٱلنَّعِيمِ ۝٨

Then you will be asked that Day about the pleasures you enjoyed.[45]

This verse shows that the servants will be asked about the pleasures they enjoyed in this world: did they show gratitude for them or not? Anyone who is required to display gratitude for every favour such as good health, sound senses, good livelihood, and, moreover, will be thoroughly examined, should know that all of his deeds taken together cannot repay even some of these favours. Hence that person would be deserving of punishment.

Kharā'iṭī, *Kitāb al-Shukr*, records on the authority of 'Abdullāh ibn 'Amr that the Prophet (ﷺ) said, "The servant will be summoned on the Day of Judgment and he will stand before Allāh, Mighty and Magnificent. He will say to His Angels, 'Look at the deeds of My servant and the favours I bestowed upon him.' They will look and say, 'They do not even amount to one of Your favours granted him.' Then He will say, 'Look to his evil deeds and good deeds.' They will look and find them the same where-

[45] *at-Takāthur* (102): 8
Tirmidhī #3358 records on the authority of Abū Hurayrah that the Prophet (ﷺ) said, "The first thing that the servant will be asked about on the Day of Judgment of the pleasures will be: Did We not give you a healthy body? Did We not give you cool water to drink?"
It was declared ṣaḥīḥ by ibn Ḥibbān #7364 and Ḥākim #7203 with Dhahabī agreeing.

upon He will say, 'Servant of Mine, I have accepted your good deeds and forgiven you your evil. My favours, I have gifted you'"[46]

Ṭabarānī records on the authority of ibn 'Umar (*raḍiyAllāhu 'anhumā*) that the Prophet (ﷺ) said, "A person will be brought on the Day of Judgment with such deeds that would burden a mountain were they to be placed on it! Then just one favour from amongst the favours of Allāh would be displayed and would almost extinguish all those deeds were Allāh not to distend them through His mercy."[47]

Ibn Abī al-Dunyā records on the authority of Anas that the Prophet (ﷺ) said, "On the Day of Judgment, blessings will be brought forward as well as good deeds and bad deeds. Allāh will say to just one of His blessings, 'Take your due from his good deeds,' and it will take all his good deeds."[48]

He also records that Wahb ibn Munabbih said, 'A servant worshipped Allāh for fifty years. Allāh inspired him with the words, "I have forgiven you." The servant asked, "Lord, what have you to forgive, I have committed no sin!" Thereupon Allāh ordered a vein in his neck to throb painfully such that he could not pray or sleep. After a while it was cured and an angel came to him, and to

---

[46] Kharā'iṭī #57.
The author, *Jāmi'*, vol. 2, p. 79, said the isnād was problematic.

[47] Ṭabarānī, *al-Awsaṭ* #1604, on the authority of ibn 'Umar.
The author, *Jāmi'*, vol. 2, p. 77, points out that the isnād has weakness as did Haythamī, vol. 10, p. 420.

[48] Ibn Abī al-Dunyā #24.
Its isnād contains a narrator who is matrūk and the author, *Jāmi'*, vol. 2, p. 78, said the isnād was ḍa'īf. However the meaning can be said to be correct.

him he complained about the vein. The angel said to him, "Your Lord, Mighty and Magnificent says: your worship for the last fifty years equates to the soothing of that vein.'"[49]

Ḥākim records on the authority of Jābir that the Prophet (ﷺ) said that Jibrīl said, "A servant worshipped Allāh on the top of a mountain, in the middle of an ocean, for five hundred years. Then he asked his Lord to let him die in the state of prostration. We used to pass by him each time we would descend and ascend and we would find written in the (pre-eternal knowledge) that he would be resurrected on the Day of Judgment and would stand before Allāh, Mighty and Magnificent. The Lord would say, 'Enter My servant into Paradise by virtue of My mercy.' The servant will say, 'My Lord, rather by virtue of my deeds!' This will happen three times, then Allāh will say to His angels, 'Weigh my favours against his deeds,' and they will find that the blessing of sight alone takes up all the deeds he did during his five hundred years of worship, with the other bodily blessings still remaining. He will say, 'Enter My servant into the Fire!' He will be dragged towards the Fire and will cry out, 'Enter me into Paradise by virtue of Your mercy! Enter me into Paradise by virtue of Your mercy!' Thereupon he shall enter Paradise." Jibrīl went on to say, "Muḥammad, things only happen by the mercy of Allāh."[50]

Whoever understands all of what has preceded will realise that his deeds, even if they are great, are not sufficient to merit his

[49] Abū Nuʿaym, vol. 4, p. 70 #4784; and ibn Abī al-Dunyā #148.

[50] Ḥākim #7637 who said it was ṣaḥīḥ but Dhahabī criticised this verdict saying that one of its narrators was not to be depended upon.

The author, *Jāmi'*, vol. 2, p. 79, points out that the ḥadīth is not authentic.

success and entry into Paradise or salvation from the Fire in and of themselves.[51] As such, he will no longer overly rely on his deeds or be impressed by them, even if they be great and wonderful. If this is the case of great and many deeds, what then would one think of the paltry deeds of the many? Such a person should ponder his deficiency in worship and devote himself to penitence and repentance!

1.6 One of the Greatest Blessings is Gratitude

As regards one whose deeds are great and many, he must busy himself with showing gratitude for them, for the accord to show gratitude is one of the greatest blessings Allāh bestows upon His servant. It is obligatory upon him to meet these deeds with gratitude and realise his deficiency in displaying due gratitude.

Wahb ibn al-Ward, when asked about the reward of a particular deed, said, 'Ask not about its reward, but ask about the gratitude due upon one who was guided to it.'[52]

Abū Sulaymān would say, 'How can an intelligent person be amazed with his deeds? Deeds are one of Allāh's blessings, as

---

[51] Aḥmad #17650 records on the authority of Muḥammad ibn Abī ʿAmīrah that the Messenger of Allāh (ﷺ) said, "Were a servant to remain in the state of prostration from the day he was born to the day he dies an old man, in devout obedience to Allāh, Mighty and Magnificent, he would consider that insignificant on the Day of Judgment and would wish to return to this world so that he may increase in reward."

It was declared ṣaḥīḥ by Albānī, *Ṣaḥīḥ al-Targhīb* #3597.

[52] Abū Nuʿaym, vol. 8, p. 155.

such it is upon him to show gratitude and to show humility. It is only the Qadariyyah who are amazed at their deeds!'[53] i.e. those who do not believe that the actions of the servant are created by Allāh, Mighty and Magnificent.

How excellent is the saying of Abū Bakr al-Nahshalī on the day that Dāwūd al-Ṭā'ī died. After his burial, ibn al-Sammāk[54] stood and praised him for his good deeds and wept causing all present to weep as well and testify to the truth of what he said... Abū Bakr al-Nahshalī stood and said, 'O Allāh, forgive him and show mercy to him and leave him not to his deeds!'[55]

Abū Dāwūd records on the authority of Zayd ibn Thābit (*raḍiyAllāhu 'anhu*) that the Messenger of Allāh (ﷺ) said, "Were Allāh to punish the inhabitants of the heavens and the inhabitants of the earth, He could do so without having oppressed them in any way. Were He to show them mercy, His mercy would be better for them than their deeds."[56]

---

[53] Ibid., vol. 9, p. 276 #13896.

[54] Ibid., vol. 8, p. 223 #11949, records that he used to say, 'Astounding it is that the eye can take delight in sleep when the Angel of Death is standing by one's pillow!'

[55] Ibid., vol. 7, p. 396 #10977.

[56] Abū Dawūd #4699 and ibn Mājah #77.
It was declared ṣaḥīḥ by ibn Ḥibbān [#727] and Albānī, *Ṣaḥīḥ al-Jāmi'* #5244
Allāh, Exalted is He says, ***"If Allāh took mankind to task by that which they deserve, He would not leave a living creature on the surface of the earth; but He grants them reprieve unto an appointed term, and when their term comes - then***

=

Ḥākim records on the authority of Jābir (*raḍiyAllāhu ʿanhu*) that a man came to the Prophet (ﷺ) and said, 'Sins, sins!' repeating this two or three times. The Messenger of Allāh (ﷺ) said, "Say: O Allāh, Your forgiveness is vaster than my sins and I have more hope in it than I do my deeds." He said this and the Messenger of Allāh (ﷺ) said, "Repeat it." He did so and he was ordered to repeat it again which he did. Then he (ﷺ) said, "Stand for you have been forgiven."[57]

My sins, were I but to ponder them, are copious.
But greater yet is my Lord's forgiveness:
In my righteous deeds lies not my expectation,
But in the mercy of Allāh have I anticipation.

1.7 Acknowledging the Grace of Allāh

Now that this noble principle has been established, it is known that deeds, in and of themselves, do not necessitate salvation from the Fire and entry into Paradise, let alone necessitating the ascension to the uppermost levels of Paradise: the levels of Those Brought Close, and seeing the face of the Lord of the worlds, and it is known that this can only come to pass through the mercy of Allāh, His grace, and forgiveness. This then requires the believer to abandon thinking highly of his deeds and to look solely

=

verily Allāh is ever Seer of His bondsmen." [*Fāṭir* (35):45]

Ibn Ḥibbān #659 records on the authority of Abū Hurayrah that the Messenger of Allāh (ﷺ) said, "Were Allāh to take me and ʿĪsā to account for our sins, He could punish us without wronging us in the least!"

It was declared ṣaḥīḥ by ibn Ḥibbān and Albānī, *Ṣaḥīḥ al-Targhīb* #2475.

[57] Ḥākim #1994.

It was declared ḍaʿīf by Albānī, *Ḍaʿīf al-Jāmiʿ* #4101.

to the grace of Allāh and His blessings.

One of the Gnostics was asked, 'Which deed is best?' He replied, 'Realising the grace of Allāh, Mighty and Magnificent.' He then recited,

If quantities were able to aid in any way,
They would join the obtuse with the judicious.

When all of this is understood, it is obligatory upon the believing the servant; the servant who desires salvation from the Fire and entry into Paradise, who desires to be close to His Master and to look on at His face; to seek all of this by taking to the means that lead to Allāh's mercy, pardon, forgiveness, pleasure, and love. It is in this way that he will attain His munificence. The means are the various deeds Allāh has appointed: only those deeds that He has legislated upon the tongue of His Messenger: only those deeds that His Messenger told us would serve to draw us closer to Allāh: those deeds that He loves and lead to His pleasure and forgiveness. Allāh, Exalted is He, says

إِنَّ رَحْمَتَ ٱللَّهِ قَرِيبٌ مِّنَ ٱلْمُحْسِنِينَ ﴿٥٦﴾

Allāh's mercy is close to the good-doers.[58]

وَرَحْمَتِي وَسِعَتْ كُلَّ شَيْءٍ فَسَأَكْتُبُهَا لِلَّذِينَ يَتَّقُونَ

My mercy extends to all things but I will prescribe it for those who have *taqwā*...[59]

[58] *al-A'rāf* (7): 56

[59] *al-A'rāf* (7): 156

So it is obligatory upon the servant to seek out those traits of *taqwā*[60] and goodness that Allāh has legislated in His Book or upon the tongue of His Messenger (ﷺ), and having done so, draw closer to Allāh, Mighty and Magnificent, through enacting them. There is no other path that can lead to the goal of the believing servant.

[60] Ṭalq ibn Ḥabīb said upon being asked about *taqwā*, 'That you perform the obedience of Allāh upon a light from Allāh, hoping for the reward of Allāh. You leave disobedience to Allāh upon a light from Allāh, fearing the punishment of Allāh.'

Recorded by ibn al-Mubārak, *al-Zuhd* #473 with a ṣaḥīḥ isnād.

Ibn al-Qayyim, *al-Risālah al-Tabūkiyyah*, p. 27, said, 'This is the best that has been said concerning the definition of *taqwā* for indeed every action must have a beginning cause to it and an objective. An action can never be considered to be obedience and a cause to draw one closer to Allāh until its point of commencement and cause be unadulterated faith, not habit, not base desires, not the wish for praise and position, nor other such things. Its objective must be the reward that lies with Allāh and His good-pleasure, this being the definition of *iḥtisāb*. This is why we often find the combined mention of these two foundations such as in his (ﷺ) saying, "Whoever fasts the month of Ramaḍān out of faith and *iḥtisāb*...".

His saying, 'upon a light from Allāh' points to the first foundation which is faith. His saying, 'hoping for the reward of Allāh' points to the second foundation which is *iḥtisāb*.'

CHAPTER TWO

The Most Beloved Deeds to Allāh

The Prophet (ﷺ) indicated the most beloved of deeds to Allāh iin the hadīths of 'Ā'ishah and Abū Hurayrah quoted at the beginning of this treatise. They are of two types:

1) Those that are done continuously and persistently, even if they be few. This was the description of the deeds of the Prophet (ﷺ), and the deeds of his family and wives after him. He would prohibit the severance of deeds saying to 'Abdullāh ibn 'Amr ibn al-'Āṣ (*raḍiyAllāhu 'anhu*), "Do not be like such-and-such a person who used to pray by night and then left it."[61]

He (ﷺ) said, "The supplication of one of you will be answered so long as he is not hasty and impatient, saying, 'I have supplicated and supplicated but have not been answered,' so he despairs and abandons the supplication."[62]

al-Ḥasan said, 'When Shayṭān looks at you and sees you persist-

[61] Bukhārī #1152 and Muslim #1159/2733.

[62] Bukhārī #6340 and Muslim#2735/6934-6936 on the authority of Abū Hurayrah.

ent in your obedience to Allāh, Mighty and Magnificent, he will do his utmost to deceive you; if he still sees you persistent, he will give up on you and leave. However, if he sees you alternating between this and that, he will have hope in you.'

2) Those deeds that are done with steadiness, balance, and ease as opposed to those that entail hardship and undue striving. Allāh, Exalted is He, says,

يُرِيدُ ٱللَّهُ بِكُمُ ٱلْيُسْرَ وَلَا يُرِيدُ بِكُمُ ٱلْعُسْرَ

Allāh desires for you ease; He desires not hardship for you.[63]

مَا يُرِيدُ ٱللَّهُ لِيَجْعَلَ عَلَيْكُم مِّنْ حَرَجٍ

Allāh does not wish to place you in a difficulty.[64]

هُوَ ٱجْتَبَىٰكُمْ وَمَا جَعَلَ عَلَيْكُمْ فِى ٱلدِّينِ مِنْ حَرَجٍ

He has chosen you and has not laid upon you in religion any hardship.[65]

The Prophet (ﷺ) would say, "Make things easy and do not make them difficult."[66]

[63] *al-Baqarah* (2): 185

[64] *al-Mā'idah* (5): 6

[65] *al-Ḥajj* (22): 78

[66] Bukhārī #3038 and Muslim #1732/4525-4526 on the authority of Abū Mūsā; Bukhārī #69, 6125 and Muslim #1734/4528 on the authority of Anas.

He (ﷺ) said, "You have been sent to make things easy, you have not been sent to make things difficult."[67]

Aḥmad records on the authority of ibn 'Abbās (*raḍiyAllāhu 'anhu*) that it was asked of the Messenger of Allāh (ﷺ), 'Which of the religions is most beloved to Allāh?' He replied, "The easy and natural religion."[68]

Aḥmad records on the authority of Miḥjan ibn al-Adrā' that the Prophet (ﷺ) entered the *Masjid* to see a man standing in prayer. He asked, "Do you think him to be truthful?" It was said, 'Prophet of Allāh, this is so-and-so, he is the best of the residents of Madīnah and the most frequent of them in prayer!' He said, "Do not let him hear you lest you render him to ruin[69] - he said it two or three times - you are a nation from whom ease is

[67] Bukhārī #220 and Abū Dāwūd #380.

[68] Aḥmad #2107 and Bukhārī, vol. 1, p. 93, as a ta'līq report.

Ar: *al-Ḥanīfiyyah al-Samḥah*. Shaykh Sindī said, 'al-Ḥanafiyyah is an attribution to the religion of Ibrāhīm and what is meant here is the religion of Islām with which our Prophet (ﷺ) was sent for it resembles the religion of Ibrāhīm in its foundations and in many of the subsidiary issues. The Ḥanīf in the language of the Arabs is one who follows the religion of the Ibrāhīm. al-Samḥah means that which is easy upon the self and not burdensome like monasticism.'

Aḥmad #24855 also records on the authority of 'Ā'ishah that the Prophet (ﷺ) said, "I have been sent with the easy religion."

[69] Bukhārī #2663-6060 records on the authority of Abū Mūsā that the Prophet (ﷺ) heard a person excessively praising another person to which he said, "You have broken his back!"

Aḥmad #5684 records on the authority of ibn 'Umar that the Prophet (ﷺ) said, "If you see those given to praising, throw dust in their faces." It was declared ṣaḥīḥ by ibn Ḥibbān #5770 and Haythamī, vol. 8, p. 117.

desired."[70]

Another narration has the wording, "The best part of your religion is the easiest of it."[71] Another narration has the wording, "You will not attain this matter through excess and trying to overcome it."[72]

This ḥadīth was also recorded by Ḥumayd ibn Zanjawayh and his version adds, "...do such actions as you are able to bear, for Allāh does not stop (rewarding you) until you grow tired and give up, and upon you is a journey [to Allāh] at the beginning of the day, at the end of the day, and a portion of the latter part of the night."[73]

Aḥmad records on the authority of Buraydah (*raḍiyAllāhu ʿanhu*) who said, 'I went out only to see the Messenger of Allāh (ﷺ), so I joined him. We saw a man in front of us praying many prayers and he (ﷺ) asked, "Do you think he is showing off?" I said,

---

[70] Aḥmad #20347.

It was declared authentic by Haythamī, vol. 3, pp. 308-310, vol. 4, p. 15.

"A nation from whom ease is desired," meaning that you have no need of going to such extremities in worship, and neither should a person be praised for doing so, rather a balanced path is more deserving.

[71] Aḥmad #18976. The meaning is that one should be balanced in actions of worship without going to extremes.

[72] Aḥmad #18971.

Bukhārī #39 records on the authority of Abū Hurayrah that the Prophet (ﷺ) said, "This religion is easy, none makes it hard except that it will overwhelm him. Therefore be firm, steadfast, and balanced..."

[73] The first part of this ḥadīth is also recorded by Bukhārī #43-1151

"Allāh and His Messenger know best." He released his hand from mine and joined both his hands together, lowering and raising them saying, "Stick to a middle path for whoever makes this religion difficult will find that it overwhelms him.'"[74]

This ḥadīth is also recorded as a mursal report and it mentions that the Prophet (ﷺ) said, "This person has taken to the way of difficulty and not to the way of ease." He then pushed the man in his chest and left and that man was not seen in the *Masjid* again.[75]

The Prophet (ﷺ) objected to those who wished to continuously live a life of a hermit, to be castrated, to pray through the whole night, fast every day, and recite the whole Qur'ān every night such as 'Abdullāh ibn 'Amr ibn al-'Āṣ, 'Uthmān ibn Maẓ'ūn, al-Miqdād, and others. He (ﷺ) said, "...but I fast, and I break my fast; I pray by night and I sleep; and I marry women: whoever turns away from my Sunnah is not of me."[76]

---

[74] Aḥmad #19786,-22963.

Ibn Khuzaymah #1179 said it was ṣaḥīḥ as did Ḥākim #1176 with Dhahabī agreeing.

The last sentence is also recorded by Aḥmad #23053 on the authority of Buraydah al-Aslamī.

[75] Aḥmad #13052 records on the authority of Anas ibn Mālik that the Messenger of Allāh (ﷺ) said, "This religion is powerful so travel through it with gentleness."

He also #1851 records on the authority of ibn 'Abbās that the Messenger of Allāh (ﷺ) said, "Beware of excessiveness in the religion for those who came before you were destroyed because of it."

[76] Abū Dāwūd #1369 on the authority of 'Ā'ishah.

He finally advised 'Abdullāh ibn 'Amr to recite the Qur'ān completely every seven days, and one narration mentions that he finally advised him to complete it once every three days. He (ﷺ) said, "The one who recites it in less than three days has not understood it." With regards fasting he (ﷺ) finally advised him with the fast of Dāwūd saying, "There is no fast better than that." With regards praying by night he (ﷺ) advised with the prayer of Dāwūd.[77]

---

[77] Bukhārī #3418 and Muslim #1159-2729-2730-2739. The fast of Dāwūd is to fast one day and not fast the next. The night prayer of Dāwūd consisted of him sleeping half the night, praying the next third, and sleeping the next sixth.

CHAPTER THREE

The Meaning of "*Saddidū wa Qāribū*"

His (ﷺ) saying in the ḥadīth of Abū Hurayrah and 'Ā'ishah, "Be firm, steadfast, and balanced,"[78] *Saddidū* means to act with firmness and fortitude. It means to take a balanced path in worship, not being deficient by leaving off what one has been commanded with, or by taking on more than one can bear. Naḍr ibn Shumayl said, '*al-sadād* means to take the path of balance in the religion.'

Similarly, *Qāribū* means the same thing: taking to a path between deficiency and excessiveness. As such they are two words carrying the same or similar meanings. This is the meaning of his (ﷺ) words in the other narration, "Stick to a middle path."

His (ﷺ) saying, "...upon which have glad tidings," means that whoever obeys Allāh upon firmness and balance, for him are glad tidings because he will reach the goal and outstrip the one who expends a great deal of effort in performing deeds. The path of balance and firmness is better than all other paths; being balanced in following the Sunnah is better than striving hard in other

[78] *Saddidū wa Qāribū*

than it, "The best guidance is the guidance of Muḥammad (ﷺ)."[79] Whoever traverses his path will find it closer to Allāh than any other path. Virtue is not attained by doing a great deal of outward deeds, rather it is attained by deeds being sincere for Allāh and being correct in that they are done in accordance to the Sunnah, and through gnosis of the heart and its actions.

Whoever has more knowledge of Allāh, His religion, and His ordinances, and has more fear, hope, and love for him is better than one who has not attained his level, even if the latter do more outward deeds. This understanding is derived from the ḥadīth of 'Ā'ishah, "Be firm, steadfast, and balanced upon which have glad tidings for indeed actions alone will not cause one to enter Paradise. The most beloved deeds to Allāh are those that are done continuously and persistently, even if they be few."

Therefore he ordered us to take a middle path in deeds and to add to this knowledge of the most beloved deeds to Allāh, and he informed us that deeds alone will not cause one entry into Paradise.

It is for this reason that some of the Salaf said, 'Abū Bakr did not outstrip you by virtue of much fasting or prayer, but rather because of something that had taken root in his heart.'[80] Some of them said, 'What was in the heart of Abū Bakr (*raḍiyAllāhu 'anhu*) was the love of Allāh and sincerity to His servants.'

Some of the Gnostics said, 'None who reached the heights did

[79] Muslim #867/2005

[80] Ḥakīm al-Tirmidhī, *al-Nawādir* as a saying of Bakr ibn 'Abdullāh al-Muzanī.

so through a great deal of fasting and prayer, rather through generosity of soul, soundness of heart, and sincerity to the nation,'[81] some added, 'and censure of their own souls.' One of them said, 'The difference in their ranking lay in their objectives and intent, not in a great deal of fasting and prayer.'

The long life of the children of Israel and their great efforts in worship was mentioned to Abū Sulaymān to which he said, 'Allāh wants from you only a truthful intention for what lies with Him,'[82] or words to that effect.

Ibn Mas'ūd said to his companions, 'You fast and pray more than the Companions of Muḥammad (ﷺ) but they were better than you.' They asked, 'How so?' He replied, 'They were more abstinent of this world than you and more desirous of the Hereafter.'[83] Hence he indicated that the superiority of the Companions lay in the attachment of their hearts to the Hereafter, their desire for it, their turning away from this world, and their thinking little of it even if it be readily available to them. Their hearts were empty of the world and filled with the Hereafter. This is what they inherited from their Prophet (ﷺ). He (ﷺ) was one whose heart was most devoid of the world and most attached to Allāh and the Abode of the Hereafter, this despite his outwardly interacting with the creation, fulfilling the duties of Prophethood, and implementing the politics of the religion and world.

---

[81] Abū Nu'aym, vol. 8, p. 103, from Fuḍayl ibn 'Iyāḍ

[82] Ibid., vol. 9, p. 263.

[83] Ibid., vol. 1, p. 136.

This was the state of the *Khulafā'* who came after him and those who followed them in goodness such as al-Ḥasan and 'Umar ibn 'Abdu'l-'Azīz. There were, in their times, those who fasted more than them and prayed more than them, but their hearts had not attained the levels of theirs in terms of leaving the world and turning to the Hereafter, and settling there.

3.1 A Noble Principle

The best of people are those who traverse the path of the Prophet (ﷺ) and the elite of his Companions such that they are moderate in the bodily actions of worship and strive to correct the affairs and states of the heart. This is because the journey to the Hereafter is cut short by the journey of the hearts, not the journey of the bodies.

A man came to one of the Gnostics and said, 'I have journeyed long and hard to reach you.' He replied, 'This matter is not about arduous journeys, rather, with one step, distance your lower self from you and then will you find the accomplishment of your objective.'

Abū Zayd said, 'I saw the Lord of Might in a dream and I asked Him, "My Lord! How does one traverse the path to You?" He replied, "Abandon your self and come with welcome!"'[84]

No nation has been given what this nation has been given and that by virtue of its following its Prophet (ﷺ). He was the best of creation and his guidance was the best of guidance, through him Allāh made the religion easy, and through him He unburdened his nation of many a hardship and difficulty. Whoever obeys

[84] Ibn al-Jawzī, *Ṣifatu'l-Ṣafwah*, vol. 4, p. 111 #179.

him has obeyed Allāh and followed His guidance, and He will, in turn, love him.

3.2 The Ease of this Religion

Some examples of the ease that resulted through his (ﷺ) blessings is that the one who prays 'Ishā in congregation, it is as if he has prayed half the night, and the one who prays Fajr in congregation, it is as if he has prayed the whole night.[85] Hence the night prayer is recorded for him while he lies asleep on his bed, and more so if he goes to sleep in a state of purity and remains in the remembrance of Allāh until his eyes close. Whoever fasts three days of every month it is as if he has fasted the whole month.[86] Hence he is regarded to be fasting the remaining days of the month in the record of Allāh even though he is eating and "the one who is eating and grateful has the reward of the one who is patiently fasting."[87] Whoever has the intention of waking up to

---

[85] Muslim #656/1491 on the authority of 'Uthmān.

Ibn al-Qayyim, *al-Manār al-Munīf*, p. 40, said, 'Therefore the one who prays these prayers in congregation has the reward of one who prayed the whole night. If this person prays these two prayers in congregation and prays by night he receives both the rewards of actually praying the night and the equivalent reward again. If this person prays those two prayers by himself but prays the night prayer will get the reward of one who had prayed in congregation and slept by night.'

[86] Bukhārī #3418 and Muslim #1159/2729

[87] Tirmidhī #2486 and Ibn Mājah #1765 on the authority of Sinān ibn Sannah.

Tirmidhī said it was ḥasan gharīb and Būṣayrī said the isnād was ṣaḥīḥ. It was declared ṣaḥīḥ by ibn Ḥibbān #315 and Ḥākim #7194 with Dhahabī agreeing.

pray by night but is overcome by sleep will have the reward of the night prayer recorded for him and that sleep of his would be a charity from Allāh.[88]

Abū'l-Dardā' said, 'Excellent indeed is the sleep of the intelligent and their breaking of fast! Look how they outstrip the night vigil and the fasting of the obtuse!'[89]

It is for this reason that the authentic ḥadīth mentions, "It is well possible that one who prays by night gets nothing from it save weariness and a person fasting gets nothing from it save hunger and thirst." Recorded by Ṭabarānī and Aḥmad.[90]

Someone said, 'Many are the ones seeking forgiveness but their lot is anger, and many are the ones who are silent but their lot is mercy. The first seeks forgiveness yet his heart remains the heart of a rebellious sinner and the second remains silent but his heart is engrossed in the remembrance of Allāh.' Another said, 'The issue is not about praying by night, rather the issue is of one who sleeps on his bed but awakes having outstripped the vanguard.' In this regard it has been said,

[88] Abū Dāwūd #1314 and ibn Mājah #1344 from Abū'l-Dardā'. 'Irāqī #1225 said the isnād was ṣaḥīḥ.

[89] Abū Nu'aym, vol. 1, p. 211.

[90] Aḥmad #8856 on the authority of Abū Hurayrah and Ṭabarānī #13413 on the authority of ibn 'Umar.

It was declared ṣaḥīḥ by ibn Khuzaymah #1997 and Ḥākim #1571 with Dhahabī agreeing. Ḥaythamī, vol. 3, p. 202, said its narrators were trustworthy and precise.

What have I to do with your faltering journey -
Walk with ease and at the fore will you be!

CHAPTER FOUR

The Meaning of "the beginning of the day", "the end of the day," & "a portion of the latter part of the night"

His (ﷺ) saying, "Journey [to Allāh] in the beginning of the day, the end of the day, and a portion of the latter part of the night" has the meaning of his (ﷺ) saying in another narrations, "Seek help in this by journeying [to Allāh] at the beginning of the day, at the end of the day and a portion of the latter part of the night."

The meaning of this is that these three periods are times of journeying to Allāh through performing actions of obedience. These are the end of the night, the beginning of the day, and the end of the day. Allāh, Exalted is He, has mentioned these times in His sayings,

وَٱذْكُرِ ٱسْمَ رَبِّكَ بُكْرَةً وَأَصِيلًا ﴿٢٥﴾
وَمِنَ ٱلَّيْلِ فَٱسْجُدْ لَهُۥ وَسَبِّحْهُ لَيْلًا طَوِيلًا ﴿٢٦﴾

Remember the name of thy Lord at morn and evening, and worship Him (a portion) of the night, and glorify Him through the livelong

night.[91]

وَسَبِّحْ بِحَمْدِ رَبِّكَ قَبْلَ طُلُوعِ ٱلشَّمْسِ وَقَبْلَ غُرُوبِهَا
وَمِنْ ءَانَآيِ ٱلَّيْلِ فَسَبِّحْ وَأَطْرَافَ ٱلنَّهَارِ لَعَلَّكَ تَرْضَىٰ ﴿١٣٠﴾

And glorify your Lord - all the while praising Him - ere the rising of the sun and ere the going down thereof. And glorify Him some hours of the night and at the two ends of the day: that you may be well pleased.[92]

وَسَبِّحْ بِحَمْدِ رَبِّكَ
قَبْلَ طُلُوعِ ٱلشَّمْسِ وَقَبْلَ ٱلْغُرُوبِ ﴿٣٩﴾ وَمِنَ ٱلَّيْلِ فَسَبِّحْهُ
وَأَدْبَـٰرَ ٱلسُّجُودِ ﴿٤٠﴾

And glorify your Lord - all the while praising Him - before the rising of the sun and before its setting; and in the night-time glorify Him, and after the (prescribed) prostrations.[93]

Allāh, Most High, mentions the remembrance of Him at the two ends of the day in numerous places in His Book such as,

يَـٰٓأَيُّهَا ٱلَّذِينَ ءَامَنُوا۟ ٱذْكُرُوا۟ ٱللَّهَ ذِكْرًا كَثِيرًا ﴿٤١﴾ وَسَبِّحُوهُ بُكْرَةً
وَأَصِيلًا ﴿٤٢﴾

---

[91] *al-Insān* (76): 25-26

[92] *Ṭa Hā* (20): 130

[93] *Qāf* (50): 39-40

O you who believe! Remember Allāh with much remembrance and glorify Him morning and evening.[94]

وَٱسْتَغْفِرْ لِذَنۢبِكَ وَسَبِّحْ بِحَمْدِ رَبِّكَ بِٱلْعَشِىِّ وَٱلْإِبْكَٰرِ ﴿٥٥﴾

And ask forgiveness for your sin, and glorify your Lord - all the while praising Him - at the fall of night and in the early hours.[95]

وَلَا تَطْرُدِ ٱلَّذِينَ يَدْعُونَ رَبَّهُم بِٱلْغَدَوٰةِ وَٱلْعَشِىِّ يُرِيدُونَ وَجْهَهُۥ

Repel not those who call upon their Lord at morn and evening, seeking His face.[96]

He said concerning the remembrance of Zakariyyah (*ʿalayhis-salām*),

فَأَوْحَىٰٓ إِلَيْهِمْ أَن سَبِّحُوا۟ بُكْرَةً وَعَشِيًّا ﴿١١﴾

...and signified to them: Glorify (your Lord) at morning and fall of night.[97]

---

[94] *al-Aḥzāb* (33): 41-42

[95] *Ghāfir* (40): 55

[96] *al-Anʿām* (6): 52

[97] *Maryam* (19): 11

وَسَبِّحْ بِٱلْعَشِيِّ وَٱلْإِبْكَٰرِ ﴿٤١﴾

...and glorify (Him) at the fall of night and in the early hours.[98]

Out of these three times there are two which are at the beginning of the day and the end of the day. At these two times one finds both obligatory and optional actions to do. The obligatory actions are the prayers of Fajr and ʿAṣr and these two are the best prayers of the five daily prayers. These are the prayers prayed "at the two cool periods," and whoever preserves these two prayers shall enter Paradise.[99] It is said about both these prayers that they are the "Middle Prayer."[100] As for the optional deed then it is to remember Allāh after the Fajr prayer until the sun rises and after ʿAṣr until the sun sets, there are many texts concerning the excellence of this. Likewise there are many texts concerning the remembrances to be said in the morning and evening and concerning the excellence of one who remembers Allāh when awaking and when sleeping.

Ibn ʿUmar reports that the Messenger of Allāh (ﷺ) said, "Son of Ādam, remember me for an hour in the beginning of the day and an hour at the end and I will forgive you your sins committed

---

[98] *Āli ʿImrān* (3): 41

[99] Bukhārī #574 and Muslim #635-1438 on the authority of Abū Mūsā

[100] mentioned in His saying, ***"Guard strictly your prayers, and the Middle Prayer."*** [*al-Baqarah* (2): 238]

Bukhārī #6396 and Muslim #627-1420-1426 record a ḥadīth stating that the Middle Prayer is the ʿAṣr prayer. The author, may Allāh have mercy upon him, also proceeds to mention other reasons that strengthen this verdict.

between them save any major sins for which you must repent."[101]

The Salaf would place greater emphasis on the end of the day than the beginning. Ibn al-Mubārak said, 'It has reached us that the one who remembers Allāh at the end of the day will be recorded as having performed remembrance throughout the day.' Abū'l-Jald said, 'It has reached us that Allāh, Exalted is He, descends to the lowest heaven during the eve of every day and looks at the deeds of the children of Ādam.'

One of the Salaf saw Abū Ja'far al-Qāri' in a dream saying to him, 'Tell Abū Ḥāzim - al-A'raj i.e. - the ascetic and highly perspicuous person - that Allāh and His Angels look to your gathering in the evenings.'[102] It seems clear that Abū Ḥāzim used to narrate stories to people at the end of the day.

A ḥadīth mentions, "Remembrance after Fajr is more beloved than freeing four slaves and remembrance after 'Aṣr is better than freeing eight slaves."[103]

The end of the day of Jumu'ah is better than its beginning due to its containing an hour wherein the supplication is answered.[104] The end of the Day of 'Arafah is better than the beginning be-

[101] Abū Nu'aym, vol. 8, p. 213, records a ḥadīth with this meaning on the authority of Abū Hurayrah and it is ḍa'īf.

[102] Ibn al-Jawzī, vol. 2, p. 167 #185.

[103] Aḥmad #22185-22254 records a ḥadīth on the authority of Abū Umāmah with the same meaning and Haythamī, vol. 10, p. 104, said that its isnāds were ḥasan.

[104] Bukhārī #935 and Muslim #852-1969-1975 on the authority of Abū Hurayrah.

cause the end of the day is the time for standing. The end of the night is better than the beginning of the night as was stated by the Salaf and they adduced the ḥadīth of the Descent as proof.[105]

All of these facts strengthen the opinion of those who say that 'Aṣr is the "Middle Prayer."

The third period is the *duljah*: journeying in the last part of the night. The meaning here is performing deeds at the end of the night which is the time for asking forgiveness. Allāh, Exalted is He says,

وَٱلْمُسْتَغْفِرِينَ بِٱلْأَسْحَارِ ﴿١٧﴾

> **And those who ask forgiveness in the early hours of the morning.**[106]

وَبِٱلْأَسْحَارِ هُمْ يَسْتَغْفِرُونَ

> **And ere the dawning of each day would seek forgiveness.**[107]

The period referred to in these verses is the last part of the

---

[105] Bukhārī #1145 and Muslim #756-1772-1778 record on the authority of Abū Hurayrah that the Messenger of Allāh (ﷺ) said, "Every night, when the last third of the night remains, our Lord, Blessed and Exalted is He, descends to the lowest heaven and says, 'Is there anyone who invokes Me that I may respond? Is there anyone asking of Me that I may give it to him? Is there anyone who asking My forgiveness that I may forgive him?'"

[106] *Āli 'Imrān* (3): 17

[107] *al-Dhāriyāt* (51): 18

time of the Descent in which Allāh fulfils the needs of those asking and grants forgiveness to the penitent. The middle of the night is reserved for the lovers who wish to spend time in intimacy with their Beloved and the end of the night is reserved for the sinners to seek forgiveness for their sins. Whoever is unable to join the striving of the lovers in the depth of the night should at least join the penitent at the end of the night.

Some narrations mention that the Throne quivers during the last part of the night. Ṭāwūs said, 'I cannot imagine that someone would sleep during the last part of the night!'[108] In a ḥadīth recorded by Tirmidhī it mentions, "Whoever fears will travel by night and whoever travels by night will reach his destination."[109]

Journeying in the last part of the night cuts short the journey of the world and the Hereafter as is mentioned in the ḥadīth recorded by Muslim, "When you journey, journey at the end of the night for the earth is compacted by night."[110]

One of the nobles said,

---

[108] ibn al-Jawzī, vol. 2, p. 285; and Abū Nu'aym, vol. 4, p. 6.

[109] Tirmidhī #2450 on the authority of Abū Hurayrah and he said it was ḥasan gharīb.

Ḥākim #7851 said it was ṣaḥīḥ and Dhahabī agreed. Albānī #3377 also declared it ṣaḥīḥ.

[110] The ḥadīth is not recorded by Muslim, rather Abū Dāwūd #2571 on the authority of Anas.

Ḥākim #1630 said it was ṣaḥīḥ and Dhahabī agreed. It was also declared ṣaḥīḥ by Albānī #3122.

The burdens of journeying by night with patience bear,
Return with the morning finding you firm in obedience.
Be not faint of heart and desist not from the aspiration
For resolve dissipates in the face of despair and exasperation.
I know - and the days have practically demonstrated -
That patience has results truly meritable.
Say: Whoever strives after a matter desired
With patience accompanying him, will surely succeed.

It is reported that al-Ashtar entered upon 'Alī ibn Abū Ṭālib (*raḍiyAllāhu 'anhu*) after resting part of the night and found him standing in prayer. He said, 'Leader of the Believers, fasting by day, praying by night, and toil between the two!' When he had finished his prayer he said, 'The journey to the Hereafter is long and it needs to be cut short by journeying by night,' - this is the *duljah*!

The wife of Ḥābib - Abū Muḥammad al-Fārisī - would wake him at night time and say, 'Awake O Ḥabīb for the path is long and our provision is paltry. The caravan of the righteous has passed ahead of us and we have been left behind!'

O sleeper by night for how long will you lie?
Awake my beloved for the Promised Time draws nigh.
For a portion of the night your Lord deify -
For sleep begets neither rest nor equanimity.
Whoever in slumber deep spends the night,
Will not have striven or arrived at the Destination right.

CHAPTER FIVE

The Meaning of Moderation

His (ﷺ) saying, "Moderation, moderation! Through this will you attain your goal!" contains encouragement towards moderation in worship such that one avoids excess and deficiency. It is for this reason that he (ﷺ) repeated it twice. al-Bazzār records the ḥadīth on the authority of Ḥudhayfah (*raḍiyAllāhu ʿanhu*) that the Prophet (ﷺ) said, "Excellent indeed is moderation in poverty. Excellent indeed is moderation in affluence. Excellent indeed is moderation in worship."[111]

Muṭarraf ibn ʿAbdullāh ibn Shikhkhīr had a son who would strive greatly in worship so he said to him, 'The best of affairs is the middle one, the good deed lies between two evil deeds and the worst of journeys is the one where one strives so much that he kills his mount and is left stranded.'[112]

Abū ʿUbaydah said: He means that excessiveness in worship is evil, deficiency is evil, and moderation is praiseworthy.

---

[111] Bazzār #2946 on the authority of Hudhayfah.
It was ruled ḍaʿīf jiddan by Albānī, *Ḍaʿīf al-Jāmiʿ* #4948.

[112] Bayhaqī #3888; and Abū Nuʿaym, vol. 2, p. 209.

This meaning is supported by the ḥadīth reported on the authority of ʿAbdullāh ibn ʿAmr (*raḍiyAllāhu ʿanhu*) that the Messenger of Allāh (ﷺ) said, "This religion is powerful so walk in it with gentleness[113] and let not the worship of Allāh become burdensome for you for the one who falters and is unable to continue has neither shortened the journey nor preserved his mount.[114] Work the deeds of a man who believes that he will die as an old man and beware of the fear of a man who believes that he will die tomorrow." Recorded by ibn Zanjawayh and others.[115]

In his (ﷺ) repeatedly mentioning the command to moderation lies an indication that one should persist in this moderation. This is because a strenuous journey in which one strives greatly is prone to end suddenly without completion; a moderate journey, however, is more likely to reach its goal. This is why the Messenger of Allāh (ﷺ) stated that the end result of moderation was the achievement of the objective, "and whoever travels by night will reach his destination."

In this world, the believer is travelling to his Lord until he reaches Him,

---

[113] This sentence was also recorded by Aḥmad #13052 on the authority of Anas ibn Mālik.
It was declared ṣaḥīḥ by Suyūṭī #2508 and ḥasan by Albānī, *Ṣaḥīḥ al-Jāmiʿ* #2246.

[114] This amount is recorded by Bazzār and Suyūṭī #2509 declared it ḍaʿīf as did Haythamī, vol. 1, p. 62.

[115] Bayhaqī, *Sunan al-Kubrā* #4520-4521, *al-Shuʿab* #3886.
ʿIrāqī #1232 said the isnād was ḍaʿīf.

يَٰٓأَيُّهَا ٱلْإِنسَٰنُ إِنَّكَ كَادِحٌ إِلَىٰ رَبِّكَ كَدْحًا فَمُلَٰقِيهِ ﴿٦﴾

You, verily, O man, are working towards your Lord - painfully toiling - and you shall meet Him.[116]

وَٱعْبُدْ رَبَّكَ حَتَّىٰ يَأْتِيَكَ ٱلْيَقِينُ ﴿٩٩﴾

And worship your Lord till the certainty comes to you.[117]

al-Ḥasan said, 'People! Persistence, persistence! Surely Allāh has appointed the time of cessation of deeds to be just before death,' and then he recited the above verse. He also said, 'Your souls are your mounts so tend to your mounts, in this way they will convey you to your Lord, Mighty and Magnificent.'

The meaning of tending to one's mounts is to be easy on them, to keep them fit and healthy, and not to overburden them. Therefore if one feels his soul is coming to a halt in its travel, he tends to it by inculcating in it the desire to finish the journey or by inculcating in it the fear of not finishing the journey, as the situation may demand. One of the Salaf said, 'Hope is the guide and fear is the driver and the soul is between the two like a headstrong animal.' So when the guide has grown tired and the driver is unable to have effect, the soul will stop and it will then need gentle treatment and "song" to provoke it into recommencing its journey. In this respect the camel leader, who drives on his herd by singing, said,

---

[116] *al-Inshiqāq* (84): 6

[117] *al-Ḥijr* (15): 99

Its guide gave it glad tidings saying:
Tomorrow shall you see bananas and mountains.

Fear is like a whip and when a person excessively whips the animal, it could well die. As such one must also strike it with "songs" of hope that would encourage it to eagerly revitalise its efforts until it arrives at the destination. Abū Yazīd said, 'I have persistently guided my soul to Allāh without letting up, it weeping all the way, then I urged it on until it laughed.'[118] It is said,

When it complained of the burdens of the journey,
he promised it
Of the relief of arrival so it revitalised its efforts.

5.1 Travelling the Path of Allāh, Mighty and Magnificent

Khulayd al-ʿAṣarī said, 'Every lover desires to meet his beloved, so love your Lord and travel to Him with a fine journey: neither arduous nor lax. This journey will take the believer to his Lord and whoever does not know the path to his Lord will not traverse it and there is no difference between such a person and an animal.'[119]

Dhū'l-Nūn said, 'The lowly are those who do not know the path to their Lord and nor do they seek to know it.'[120]

---

[118] ibn Mulaqqin, *Ṭabaqāt al-Awliyā'*, p. 278 #117.

[119] Abū Nuʿaym, vol. 2, p. 232.

[120] Ibid., vol. 9, p. 372.

The path to Allāh is to traverse His Straight Path with which He sent His Messenger (ﷺ) and for which He revealed His Book.[121] It is this Path that He commanded the whole of creation to traverse. Ibn Mas'ūd said, 'The Straight Path: Muḥammad (ﷺ) left us on one end of it and the other end is in Paradise. To its right and left are paths branching off on which stand people summoning those who pass by them. Whoever takes to those paths will end up in the Fire but the one who remains on the Path will end up in Paradise.' Then he recited,

وَأَنَّ هَٰذَا صِرَٰطِي مُسْتَقِيمًا فَٱتَّبِعُوهُ ۖ وَلَا تَتَّبِعُوا۟ ٱلسُّبُلَ فَتَفَرَّقَ بِكُمْ عَن سَبِيلِهِۦ ۚ ذَٰلِكُمْ وَصَّىٰكُم بِهِۦ لَعَلَّكُمْ تَتَّقُونَ ﴿١٥٣﴾

And verily this is My Straight Path, so follow it. Follow not other ways, lest you be parted from His way. This has He ordained for you, that you may ward off (evil).[122]

[121] Tirmidhī #76 records on the authority of Nawwās ibn Sam'ān that the Messenger of Allāh (ﷺ) said, "Allāh has set forth the following as a parable: there is a road that leads straight to the destination. On either side of the road there is a wall in which there are open doors with curtains hanging on them. From the remote end of the road, a voice calls, 'Proceed straight and do not turn aside.' Whenever someone intends to lift a curtain from the door another voice calls from above, 'Beware! Do not lift the curtain; otherwise you will be lured inside.' The Prophet (ﷺ) explained the parable by saying that the straight path is Islām, the walls are the limits imposed by Allāh, the open doors are the things that he has prohibited, the voice which calls from the end of the road is the Qur'ān and the voice which calls from above is Allāh's monitor in the heart of every believer."

It was declared ḥasan gharīb by Tirmidhī and ṣaḥīḥ by Ḥākim #245 with Dhahabī agreeing and Albānī, *Ṣaḥīḥ al-Jāmi'* #3887.

[122] *al-An'ām* (6): 153

This was recorded by ibn Jarīr and others.[123] Therefore the Path that leads to Allāh is one, the Straight Path, and all other paths are the paths of Shayṭān, whoever traverses them is cut off from Allāh and will end up in the abode of His displeasure, anger, and punishment.[124]

---

[123] Ṭabarī #14175.

[124] Ibn al-Qayyim said, 'We will expound upon the Straight Path in a succinct manner for the people have explained it in various ways all of them revolving around one essential fact. The Straight Path is the path of Allāh which He has put in place to lead mankind to Him; there is no path to Him other than this one which He appointed upon the tongues of His Messengers. It is to single Him out alone for worship and to single out His Messengers alone for obedience. Therefore none should commit *shirk* in His worship just as none should commit *shirk* in the following of His Messenger (ﷺ); one should purify his *tawḥīd* and purify his following of the Messenger (ﷺ), this is the full import of the testification that, 'None has the right to be worshipped save Allāh and Muḥammad is the Messenger of Allāh.' All of the various explanations given to the Straight Path fall under these two principles. You must love Him with all your heart, you must try to please Him to the utmost of your ability; there should not be any area of your heart except that it is overflowing with love of Him and you should have no desire except to please Him. The first point is realised through actualising, 'None has the right to be worshipped save Allāh' and the second point is realised through actualising, 'Muḥammad is the Messenger of Allāh.' This is guidance and the religion of truth, this is knowing the truth and acting upon it, this in turn is knowing what He sent His Messenger with and living by it. All definitions revolve around this essential concept. Sahl bin 'Abdullāh said, 'Stick to the narrations and Sunnah for I fear that a time will come when the Prophet (ﷺ) and the importance of following him in everything is mentioned, the people would censure the person who says this, cause others to flee from him, disassociate themselves from him, humiliate him and disgrace him.' - 'Abdu'l-Raḥmān Āli al-Shaykh, *Fatḥ al-Majīd Sharḥ Kitāb at-Tawḥīd*, p. 24.

5.2 Deeds are by their Conclusion

It is possible that a man traverse the Straight Path in the beginning of his life, then deviate from it and travel one of the paths of Shayṭān, hence he is cut off from Allāh and destroyed. "Indeed one of you will work the deeds of the People of Paradise until there is only a cubit or fathom between him and it and then he will work the deeds of the denizens of the Fire and enter it."[125]

Conversely it is possible that a person travel one of the paths of the Shayṭān in the beginning of his life and then good fortune come his way, and he traverse the Straight Path and thereby reach Allāh. It is essential that a person firmly traverse the Straight Path from the beginning of the journey to the end,

ذَٰلِكَ فَضْلُ ٱللَّهِ يُؤْتِيهِ مَن يَشَآءُ

That is the bounty of Allāh which He gives unto whom He will.[126]

وَٱللَّهُ
يَدْعُوٓا۟ إِلَىٰ دَارِ ٱلسَّلَٰمِ وَيَهْدِى مَن يَشَآءُ إِلَىٰ صِرَٰطٍ مُّسْتَقِيمٍ ﴿٢٥﴾

And Allāh summons to the Abode of Peace, and leads whom He will to a straight path.[127]

---

[125] Bukhārī #3332-6594 and Muslim #2643-6723 on the authority of ibn Masʿūd.

[126] *al-Jumuʿah* (62): 4

[127] *Yūnus* (10): 25

Many are the people who turn back after having travelled part of the journey and give up. The hearts are between two fingers of the fingers of the All-Merciful,[128]

يُثَبِّتُ ٱللَّهُ ٱلَّذِينَ ءَامَنُوا۟ بِٱلْقَوْلِ ٱلثَّابِتِ

Allāh confirms those who believe by a firm saying.[129]

My beloved! Those who falter in the path across the desert
Are many, but those who reach the end are few.

5.3 The Excellence of Drawing Close to Allāh

The ḥadīth qudsī mentions, "Whoever draws close to me by a hand-span length I draw closer to him by a cubit. Whoever draws closer to me by a cubit, I draw closer to him by a fathom. Whoever comes to Me walking, I go to Him running."[130] The narration of Aḥmad adds, "And Allāh is more exalted and greater; Allāh is more exalted and greater."[131] Another ḥadīth in Aḥmad has that Allāh, Mighty and Magnificent says, "Son of Ādam, stand before me and I will walk to you. Walk towards Me and I will run

---

128 Muslim #2654-6750 and Tirmidhī #2140.

129 *Ibrāhīm* (14): 27

130 Bukhārī #7405 and Muslim #2687-6833-2743-6952 on the authority of Abū Hurayrah.

131 Aḥmad #21374 on the authority of Abū Dharr.
Haythamī, vol. 10, p. 197, said the isnād was ḥasan.

towards you."[132]

Whoever turns towards Us,
We receive him willingly from afar
Whoever desires what We want,
We desire what he wants
Whoever asks of Us
We shall grant him more and more again
Whoever works seeking Our aid,
We will make soft for him iron.

Man! Were you to go to the door of the governor, he would not receive you or give you any attention, perhaps he will even prevent you from getting near him. But the King of kings is saying, "Whoever comes to me walking, I will go to him running," yet you turn away from Him and run after another! You have been cheated in the worst of manners and you have lost out in the severest of ways!

By Allāh, I have never come to visit you
Except that I found the earth compacting for me,
And never have I resolved to leave your door
Except that I tripped over my own garments!

O you who desire to meet Him, the path has been made clear so why the tarrying and the holding back?

The Path has been made clear to you, truly
So none who desires You need now to seek.

[132] Aḥmad #15925 on the authority of one of the Companions.
Haythamī, vol. 10, p. 197, said the narrators of the isnād were trustworthy and precise. Mundhirī, *Targhīb* #4771 said the isnād was ṣaḥīḥ as did Albānī #3153.

أَفِي ٱللَّهِ شَكٌّ فَاطِرِ ٱلسَّمَٰوَٰتِ وَٱلْأَرْضِ يَدْعُوكُمْ لِيَغْفِرَ لَكُم مِّن ذُنُوبِكُمْ

Can there be doubt concerning Allāh, the Creator of the heavens and the earth? He calls you that He may forgive you your sins.[133]

يَٰقَوْمَنَآ أَجِيبُوا۟ دَاعِيَ ٱللَّهِ

O our people! Respond to Allāh's summoner...[134]

O soul, woe to You!
Guidance has come to you,
Answer it! Here is the caller of Allāh
summoning you.
Many-a-time are you called to guidance
yet turn away do you,
But answer do you the caller to misguidance
when he calls you!

[133] *Ibrāhīm* (14): 10

[134] *al-Aḥqāf* (46): 31

5.4 The Types of Reaching Allāh

Reaching Allāh is of two types, one that occurs in this world and one that occurs in the Hereafter. The meaning of reaching in this world is that the heart attains cognisance of Him, and when it does so, it loves Him, takes solace with Him, realises His closeness to it, and finds Him readily answering its supplications. One narration mentions, "Son of Ādam, seek Me and you will find Me. When you find Me you will have found everything, and if you do not find Me, you will have lost everything."

Seek Us and you will find Us.
In hearts large enough to contain Us:
Patient and content
With all that comes to them from Us.

Dhū'l-Nūn would go out by night and frequently look up at the sky and say the following lines of poetry until morning,

Seek for yourselves
The likes of what I have found.
I have found a place of rest wherein
He never falters in His love:
If I move away, He draws me close
And if I move closer, He draws nigh.[135]

Reaching in the Hereafter means entering Paradise: the abode of Allāh's grace. However Paradise is of many levels and the closeness of its inhabitants to Allāh will depend upon the level of cognisance realised in their hearts in this world, their close-

[135] Abū Nuʿaym, vol. 9, p. 357 #14112.

ness and their witnessing,

وَكُنتُمْ أَزْوَاجًا ثَلَاثَةً ﴿٧﴾ فَأَصْحَابُ الْمَيْمَنَةِ مَا أَصْحَابُ الْمَيْمَنَةِ ﴿٨﴾ وَأَصْحَابُ الْمَشْأَمَةِ مَا أَصْحَابُ الْمَشْأَمَةِ ﴿٩﴾ وَالسَّابِقُونَ السَّابِقُونَ ﴿١٠﴾ أُولَٰئِكَ الْمُقَرَّبُونَ ﴿١١﴾

And you will be three kinds: (First) the Companions of the Right Hand; what of the Companions of the Right Hand? And (then) the Companions of the Left Hand; what of the Companions of the Left Hand? And the Foremost in the race, the Foremost in the race: Those are they who will be brought nigh.[136]

While in his house, Shiblī would become agitated and recite the following couplets,

One cannot be patient when You are afar
When to closeness is he familiar.
From You one cannot suffer being veiled
When in love is he immersed.
Even if the eye does not see You,
For sure the heart beholds You.

[136] *al-Wāqi'ah* (56): 7-11

CHAPTER SIX

Islām, Īmān, Iḥsān

In this world, the Straight Path comprises three levels: Islām, Īmān, and Iḥsān. Whoever remains on the level of Islām until he dies will be saved from eternity in the Fire and he must enter Paradise, even if, before this, he is punished in the Fire. Whoever remains on the level of Īmān until he dies will be prevented from entering the Fire altogether for the light of faith extinguishes the blaze of the Fire to such an extent that it says, 'O believer, go on your way! Your light has extinguished my blaze!'[137]

Aḥmad has the ḥadīth on the authority of Jābir that the Messenger of Allāh (ﷺ) said, "There is no righteous person or sinner except that he will enter it. It will be a source of coolness and peace for the believer just as it was for Ibrāhīm to the point that the Fire itself will raise a hue and cry at its coolness!"[138] This is the legacy of the lovers inherited from Ibrāhīm (*'alayhis-salām*).

---

[137] Ṭabarānī, *al-Kabīr* #668.

Haythamī, vol. 10, p. 360, mentions that its isnād contains a weak narrator and it was declared ḍa'īf by Suyūṭī #3354 and Albānī, *Ḍa'īf al-Jāmi'* #2474.

[138] Aḥmad #14520.

Bayhaqī #370 said that its isnād was ḥasan. Ḥākim #8744 said it was ṣaḥīḥ and =

In the fire of the lover is a blaze of love:
The fiercest heat of Hell is its coolest portion!

Whoever remains on the level of Iḥsān until he dies will reach Allāh,

لِّلَّذِينَ أَحْسَنُوا۟ ٱلْحُسْنَىٰ وَزِيَادَةٌ

For those who do good is the best (reward) and an addition.[139]

The authentic ḥadīth mentions, "When the People of Paradise enter Paradise a caller will announce, 'People of Paradise, Allāh has given you a promise which He wishes to fulfil.' They will say, 'What is that? Has He not made our faces white? Has He not made our scales heavy? Has He not granted us entry in Paradise and saved us from the Fire?' So He will remove the veil and they will look on at Him and by Allāh, He will not have granted them anything more beloved to them than this, and there will be nothing that gives more pleasure to their eyes than this! This is the addition." Then He recited the above verse.[140]

All the inhabitants of Paradise will have a share of this vision but they will differ as to their closeness when seeing Him and in

=
Dhahabī agreed. Haythamī, vol. 7, p. 55, said that the narrators of Aḥmad were trustworthy and precise. However both Albānī, *Ḍaʿīf al-Targhīb* #2110 and Arnaʾūṭ, *Taḥqīq Musnad* show that the isnād is ḍaʿīf due to the presence of an unknown narrator.

[139] *Yūnus* (10): 26

[140] Muslim #181-449 and ibn Mājah #187.

the number of times they see Him. All of the People of Paradise will see Him on the Day of Increase which is the Day of Jumu'ah,[141] and the elite amongst them will look at the Face of Allāh twice a day, once in the morning and once in the evening. The generality of the People of Paradise have their provision given them twice a day, in the morning and the evening, whereas the elite see Him in the morning and the evening. Neither palaces can make the Gnostics forget their beloved and nor can running rivers quench their thirst. One of them used to say, 'When I am hungry, remembrance of Him is my food, and when I am thirsty, witnessing Him is my wish and gratification.'[142]

One of the righteous was seen in a dream and he was asked about the condition of two scholars to which he replied, 'At this time I have left them before Allāh, Mighty and Magnificent, eating, drinking, enjoying bliss.' He was asked, 'What of you?' He

[141] Ṭabarānī, *al-Awsaṭ* #2084 on the authority of Anas.

Haythamī, vol. 2, p. 164, said that the isnād contains trustworthy and precise narrators.

[142] Ibn Abī'l-'Izz, *Sharḥ 'Aqīdah al-Ṭaḥāwiyyah*, p. 213, said, 'The nation is agreed that Allāh will not be seen by anyone in this world. They did not differ over this except with regards our Prophet (ﷺ) specifically.'

Nawawī, *Sharḥ Muslim*, vol. 2, p. 105, said, 'As for seeing Allāh, Exalted is He, in this world then we have previously mentioned that this is a possibility, however the majority of the Salaf and later generations, both amongst the Mutakallimīn and others, are of the opinion that it will not occur in this world.'

Kilābādhī, *al-Ta'arruf li Madhab al-Taṣawwuf*, p. 43, said, 'They have all agreed that He will not be seen in this world, not with the eyes nor the hearts, except from the perspective of certainty. This is because this seeing is from the greatest of blessings and as such is befitting that it occur in the best of places. Now if they were granted this vision, the greatest blessing, in this world, there would be no distinction between it and Paradise.'

Perhaps these words serve to clarify the meaning of the words of the author, may Allāh have mercy upon him.

replied, 'He knows my lack of desire for food so instead He allows me to look at Him.'

When I desire drink, You are my satiation
And when I desire food, You are my gratification.

Aḥmad records the ḥadīth on the authority of ibn 'Umar that the Messenger of Allāh (ﷺ) said, "The people with the lowest ranking in Paradise will look at his dominion for two thousand years seeing the farthest end of it as he sees the nearest end of it, and he will look at his wives and servants. The ones with the highest ranking will look at the Face of Allāh, Blessed and Exalted is He, twice a day."[143] This ḥadīth was also recorded by Tirmidhī with the wording, "The person with the lowest ranking in Paradise will be one who will look at his gardens, wives, blessings, servants, and couches, for the journey of one thousand years. The best of them with Allāh will look at His Face morning and evening."[144] Then the Messenger of Allāh (ﷺ) recited,

وُجُوهٌ يَوْمَئِذٍ نَّاضِرَةٌ ﴿٢٢﴾ إِلَىٰ رَبِّهَا نَاظِرَةٌ ﴿٢٣﴾

That Day will faces be resplendent, looking toward their Lord.[145]

It is because of this that the Messenger of Allāh (ﷺ) said in the

---

[143] Aḥmad [#5317]
Haythamī, vol. 10, p. 401, said it contains a narrator who is agreed to be ḍa'īf and Albānī, *Ḍa'īf al-Jāmi'* #1381 ruled it ḍa'īf.

[144] Tirmidhī #2553-3330 and he said it was gharīb.
It was declared ḍa'īf by Albānī, *Ḍa'īf al-Jāmi'* #1382.

[145] *al-Qiyāmah* (75): 22-23

authentic ḥadīth reported on the authority of Jarīr ibn 'Abdullāh al-Bajalī, "You will see your Lord on the Day of Judgment like you see the moon on a night when it is full, you will have no difficulty in seeing Him." He then said, "So if you are able not to be overwhelmed to the point of missing a prayer before the rising of the sun and before its setting, then do so." Then he recited,

وَسَبِّحْ بِحَمْدِ رَبِّكَ قَبْلَ طُلُوعِ ٱلشَّمْسِ وَقَبْلَ ٱلْغُرُوبِ ﴿٣٩﴾

And glorify your Lord - all the while praising Him - before the rising of the sun and before its setting.[146]

[146] *Qāf* (50): 39

Bukhārī #573 and Muslim #633-1434.

"You will not be harmed in seeing Him," the ḥadīth has two readings, one of them meaning that 'you will not be crowded so close together so you have difficulty in seeing Him' and the other meaning 'you will not be wronged in any way when you see Him such that some can see and others cannot.' - ibn al-Athīr, *al-Nihāyah*, vol. 3, pp. 92-93,

6.1 The Periods of Morning and Evening

In Paradise, these two periods are reserved for looking at Allāh with respect to the elite, and in this world he (ﷺ) encouraged the preservation of the prayer at these two times. Therefore whoever prays these two prayers in this world in the best of ways, with submissiveness, presence of heart, and performing all its mannerisms, it is hoped that he will be of those who will see Allāh at these two periods in Paradise. This is more so if one holds fast to the remembrances and other types of worship until the sun rises or sets. If the servant adds to this a journey in the last part of the night, then he has journeyed in all three times: the end of the night, the morning, and the evening, and if he is true, for sure this will be followed by the achievement of the greatest objective,

فِي مَقْعَدِ صِدْقٍ عِندَ مَلِيكٍ مُّقْتَدِرٍ ﴿٥٥﴾

In an Assembly of Truth, in the presence of a Sovereign Omnipotent.[147]

Whoever adheres resolutely to truthfulness in his journey will be led to a Sure Footing,

وَبَشِّرِ ٱلَّذِينَ ءَامَنُوٓا۟ أَنَّ لَهُمْ قَدَمَ صِدْقٍ عِندَ رَبِّهِمْ

And bring unto those who believe the good tidings that they have a sure footing with their Lord.[148]

[147] *al-Qamar* (54): 55

[148] *Yūnus* (10): 2

The lover is always asking after his beloved, inquiring about any news concerning him, eliciting any small piece of information, and following his tracks in order to traverse the path that leads to him.

O seeker after her! Is there anyone who can answer (me)?
For, after our time together, I know of no other felicity!
Were I only to know where her family have pitched tent,
To which of Allāh's lands have they wandered to,
We would have rushed after her as does the wind!
Seeking this felicity even if it be beyond the stars!

Great indeed is the aspiration whose goal is Allāh and noble indeed is the soul whose beloved is He.

Allāh says,

وَلَا تَطْرُدِ ٱلَّذِينَ يَدْعُونَ رَبَّهُم بِٱلْغَدَوٰةِ وَٱلْعَشِيِّ يُرِيدُونَ وَجْهَهُۥ

Repel not those who call upon their Lord at morn and evening, seeking His face.[149]

What has the lover to do save the pursuit of his love?
In every land the lover roams as one delirious.

[149] *al-Anʿām* (6): 52

6.2 Those who Hold to the World and those who Hold on to the Hereafter

The worth of every man is judged by what he seeks. None can put a value to one who seeks Allāh for this is immeasurable. The one who seeks after the world is too lowly to be valued. Shiblī said, 'Whoever holds fast to this world will be burned by its blaze until he becomes ashes blown about by the wind. Whoever holds on to the Hereafter will be burned by its light such that he becomes pure gold of the highest quality and is benefited from. Whoever holds on to Allāh will be burned by the light of Tawḥīd and will become a jewel that is beyond value.'

He has ambitions, the greatest of which is illimitable;
The least of which time itself finds untouchable.

al-Shiblī was asked, 'Will the lover ever gain satisfaction from something from his Beloved before witnessing Him?' He replied with the following couplets,

By Allāh! Were You to crown me
With the crown of Chosroes, king of the orient,
And before me the wealth of creation present -
The wealth of those today and those of old -
'But we shall not meet for a time,' I am told
To our meeting, My Master, would I gladly assent!

Whoever's ambition is great will only ever be content with seeking Allāh, Glorious and Exalted is He.

My every journey to and fro,
Morning and evening -

And so too, remembrance of You
- is my very breath of life,
A refreshing breeze and soothing quietude.
You are my ambition and my lot,
My objective and my success.
O source of my succour and refuge
Keep me guided aright and correct me

CHAPTER SEVEN

The Unexpected Confrontation

Allāh, Exalted is He says,

وَبَدَا لَهُم مِّنَ ٱللَّهِ مَا لَمْ يَكُونُوا۟ يَحْتَسِبُونَ ﴿٤٧﴾

And there will appear unto them, from their Lord, that wherewith they never reckoned.[150]

This verse bore down heavily upon the fearful Gnostics for it states that some servants, when they meet Allāh, will be confronted with things that they never expected. For example he could be unaware of what his hands have wrought, not paying it any attention, then when his covering is lifted he will see these terrible matters, and have things confront him that he never catered for. This is why 'Umar (*raḍiyAllāhu 'anhu*) said, 'If I had the dominion of the whole earth I would gladly ransom it to save me from the terror of the unveiling.'[151] A ḥadīth mentions, "Hope not for death for the terror of the unveiling is great. It is from the

[150] *Zumar* (39): 47

[151] Abū Ya'lā #2731, and Haythamī, vol. 9, pg. 77 said that its narrators were those of the Ṣaḥīḥ, and Abū Nu'aym, vol. 1, p. 52.

felicity of a person that Allāh grant him long life and nourish him with penitence."[152]

One of the sages amongst the Salaf said, 'How many occasions of sorrow will one face on the Day of Judgment that did not even cross his mind.' In this vein Allāh, Exalted is He says,

لَّقَدْ كُنتَ فِي غَفْلَةٍ مِّنْ هَٰذَا فَكَشَفْنَا عَنكَ غِطَاءَكَ فَبَصَرُكَ الْيَوْمَ حَدِيدٌ

You were in heedlessness of this. Now We have removed from your covering from you, and piercing is your sight this Day.[153]

7.1 The Types of Actions that will be as Scattered Dust

The First: comprising something more general than previously mentioned and that is one having deeds from which he hopes good but they end up scattered dust and are altered to evil deeds. Allāh, Exalted is He says,

وَالَّذِينَ كَفَرُوا أَعْمَالُهُمْ كَسَرَابٍ
بِقِيعَةٍ يَحْسَبُهُ الظَّمْآنُ مَاءً حَتَّىٰ إِذَا جَاءَهُ لَمْ يَجِدْهُ شَيْئًا
وَوَجَدَ اللَّهَ عِندَهُ فَوَفَّاهُ حِسَابَهُ وَاللَّهُ سَرِيعُ الْحِسَابِ ﴿٣٩﴾

---

[152] Aḥmad #14564 on the authority of Jābir.
Haythamī, vol. 10, p. 204, said the isnād was ḥasan as did Mundhirī #5098.

[153] *Qāf* (50): 22

As for those who disbelieve, their deeds are as a mirage in a desert. The thirsty one thinks it to be water till he comes to it and finds it naught, and finds, in the place thereof, Allāh Who will pay him his due; and Allāh is swift at reckoning.[154]

وَقَدِمْنَآ إِلَىٰ مَا عَمِلُوا۟ مِنْ عَمَلٍ فَجَعَلْنَـٰهُ هَبَآءً مَّنثُورًا ﴿٢٣﴾

And We shall turn unto the work they did and make it scattered motes.[155]

Fuḍayl said concerning this verse, ***"And there will appear unto them, from their Lord, that wherewith they never reckoned,"*** 'They worked deeds thinking them to be good when in reality they were evil.'

The Second: Close to the above: a servant commits an evil deed to which he pays no regard, thinking it insignificant, and that sin will be the cause of his perdition as Allāh says,

وَتَحْسَبُونَهُۥ هَيِّنًا وَهُوَ عِندَ ٱللَّهِ عَظِيمٌ ﴿١٥﴾

...you counted it a trifle but in the sight of Allāh it is very great. [156]

One of the Companions said, 'You are doing deeds that are, in your eyes, more insignificant than a hair, whereas at the time of the Messenger of Allāh (ﷺ) we would consider them to be de-

[154] *an-Nūr* (24): 39

[155] *al-Furqān* (25): 23

[156] *an-Nūr* (24): 15

structive sins!'[157]

The Third: Worse than the previous case: one to whom the evil of his conduct seems pleasing. Allāh, Exalted is He says,

قُلْ هَلْ نُنَبِّئُكُم بِٱلْأَخْسَرِينَ
أَعْمَـٰلًا ﴿١٠٣﴾ ٱلَّذِينَ ضَلَّ سَعْيُهُمْ فِى ٱلْحَيَوٰةِ ٱلدُّنْيَا وَهُمْ يَحْسَبُونَ أَنَّهُمْ
يُحْسِنُونَ صُنْعًا ﴿١٠٤﴾

> **Say: Shall We inform you who will be the greatest losers by their works? Those whose efforts go astray in the life of the world, and yet they reckon that they do good work.**[158]

ibn 'Uyaynah said, 'When death came to Muḥammad ibn al-Munkadir he became apprehensive and so the people summoned Abū Ḥāzim and he came. Ibn al-Munkadir said to him, "Allāh says, ***'And there will appear unto them, from their Lord, that wherewith they never reckoned,'*** and I fear that things will become clear to me and confront me that I never expected." Then both of them broke down in tears.' Recorded by ibn Abī Ḥātim and ibn Abī al-Dunyā adds in his report, 'So his family said, "We called you that you may console him but you have only increased his apprehension!" He then told them of what he had said.'[159]

Fuḍayl ibn 'Iyāḍ said, 'I have been informed that it was said to Sulaymān al-Taymī, "You! Who is there like you!" He said, "Quiet!

---

[157] Bukhārī #6492 on the authority of Anas.

[158] *Kahf* (18): 103-104

[159] ibn al-Jawzī, vol. 2, p. 167 #185.

Do not say this! I do not know what will appear before me from Allāh, I have heard Allāh saying, ***"And there will appear unto them, from their Lord, that wherewith they never reckoned."'***[160]

The Fourth: Sufyān al-Thawrī would say upon hearing this verse, 'Woe to the people of ostentation.'[161] This can be seen in the ḥadīth about the three who would be the first to be hurled into the Fire: the scholar, the one who gave charity, and the mujāhid.[162]

---

[160] Dhahabī, *Tadhkiratu'l-Ḥuffāẓ*, vol. 1, p. 151.

[161] Qurṭubī, vol. 15, p. 265.

[162] Muslim #1905/4923 on the authority of Abū Hurayrah with the words, 'The first man (whose case) will be decided on the Day of Judgment, will be a man who died as a martyr. He shall be brought forth and Allāh will recount His blessings (which He had bestowed upon him) and he will acknowledge them. Then Allāh will ask, "What did you do with them?" He will reply, "I fought for Your sake until I died as a martyr." Allāh will say, "You lie. You fought so that you might be called a 'brave warrior' and you were called so." Then a command will be given and he will be dragged on his and cast into Hell.

And a man who acquired knowledge and taught it and recited the Qur'ān. He will be brought forth and Allāh will recount His blessings (which He had bestowed upon him) and he will acknowledge them. Then Allāh will ask, "What did you do with them?" He will say, "I acquired knowledge and disseminated it and recited the Qur'ān for your sake." Allāh will say, "You lie. You acquired knowledge so that you might be called 'a scholar,' and you recited the Qur'ān so that it might be said, 'He is a Qāri',' and it was said. Then a command will be given and he will be dragged on his and cast into Hell.

And a man whom Allāh had made abundantly rich and had granted every kind of wealth. He will be brought forth and Allāh will recount His blessings (which He had bestowed upon him) and he will acknowledge them. Then Allāh will ask, "What did you do with them?" He will say, "I spent money in every cause in which You wished that it should be spent for Your sake." Allāh will say, "You lie. You did so that it might be said, "He is generous," and it was said. Then a command will be given and he will be dragged on his and cast into Hell.'

The Fifth: The one who has worked righteous deeds but has also wronged others and he thinks that his deeds will save him, so there confronts him that which he was not expecting. All of his deeds are apportioned amongst those who he wronged, then some wrong still remains to be requited, and so their evil deeds are piled onto his and as a result he is hurled into the Fire.[163]

The Sixth: His account could be scrutinised at which it will be asked of him to show how he was grateful for the blessings granted him. The least blessing would be balanced against his deeds and outweigh them with the remaining blessings yet to be weighed! This is why the Prophet (ﷺ) said, "Whoever's account is scrutinised will be punished," or, "will be destroyed."[164]

The Seventh: He could have evil deeds that destroy some of his deeds or the deeds of his limbs, save Tawḥīd, as a result of which he will enter the Fire. Ibn Mājah records the ḥadīth on the authority of Thawbān that the Messenger of Allāh (ﷺ) said, "There are people amongst my nation who will come with deeds like mountains and Allāh will render them as scattered dust." This ḥadīth goes on to mention, "They are a people who have your skin, (they speak your language),[165] they spend part of the night in prayer as you do, but they are people who, when they are alone, violate the prohibitions of Allāh."[166]

---

[163] See the ḥadīth in fn. #34

[164] See fn. #36-38

[165] This sentence is not found in the ḥadīth of ibn Mājah.

[166] Ibn Mājah #4245.
Būṣayrī said, 'Its isnād is ṣaḥīḥ' and it was declared ṣaḥīḥ by Albānī, #2346.

Yaʿqūb ibn Shaybah and ibn Abī al-Dunyā record on the authority of Sālim, the freed-slave of Abū Ḥudhayfah, that the Messenger of Allāh (ﷺ) said, "A group of people will be brought on the Day of Judgment with deeds like Mount Tihāmah and Allāh will render their deeds to dust and they will be thrown face first in the Fire." Sālim said, 'I fear that I am one of them!' He (ﷺ) said, "They would fast, pray, and apportion some of the night for worship, but in secret, when an opportunity to do something forbidden presented itself, they would take it and as such Allāh will invalidate their deeds." A person could have his deeds annulled because of showing off or arrogance and the likes yet not even be aware of it!

7.2 Sadness in the World & Misery in the Hereafter

Ḍaygam, the devout worshipper, said, 'If the Hereafter of the believer does not bring happiness then two matters have gathered for him: sadness in this world and misery in the Hereafter.' It was asked of him, 'How can a person who is striving hard in the abode of this world not face happiness in the Hereafter?' He replied, 'What of acceptance? What of safety? How many are the people who think they have worked righteous deeds yet on the Day of Judgment they are gathered together and thrown in his face.'[167]

It is because of this that 'Āmir ibn 'Abd Qays and others would be greatly apprehensive of the verse,

إِنَّمَا يَتَقَبَّلُ ٱللَّهُ مِنَ ٱلْمُتَّقِينَ ﴿٢٧﴾

> **Allāh accepts only from those who ward off (evil).**[168]

Ibn 'Awn said, 'Do not feel secure because of a great number of deeds for you do not know if they have been accepted or not. Do not feel secure about your sins for you do not know if they have been expiated or not. This is because all of your deeds are unseen to you and you have no idea what Allāh will do with them.'

---

[167] Abū Nu'aym, vol. 3, p. 360.

[168] *al-Mā'idah* (5): 27

Nakhaʿī wept at the time of his death saying, 'I await the messenger of my Lord and I have no idea if he will give me glad tidings of Paradise or Hell.'[169] Another also felt anxious at the time of death and it was asked of him, 'Why so anxious?' He replied, 'This is the time in which I have no idea where I will be led.'

One of the Companions was overcome with anxiety at the time of his death and he was asked after his state to which he replied, 'Allāh took His creation in two handfuls, a handful for Paradise and a handful for Hell, and I have no idea to which handful I belong!'[170]

[169] Abū Nuʿaym, vol. 4, p. 224.

[170] Aḥmad #17594 on the authority of one of the Companions, and Haythamī, vol. 7, pg. 187 said, 'Its narrators are those of the Ṣaḥīḥ.' Ṭabarānī, *al-Kabīr*, vol. 20, pg. 365, records it on the authority of Muʿādh ibn Jabal and Haythamī points out two weaknesses in the isnād.

7.3 Beware, beware!

Whoever ponders this as it deserves will find himself in a state of apprehension for the son of Ādam will face great terrors during his life such as death, the grave, the barzakh,[171] the Standing; the Bridge and the Balance, and the greatest of all: standing before Allāh, Mighty and Magnificent, and the Fire. He will fear losing his faith at the last minute and being condemned for eternity in the Fire. The true believer will never feel secure from all these matters,

فَلَا يَأْمَنُ مَكْرَ ٱللَّهِ إِلَّا ٱلْقَوْمُ ٱلْخَٰسِرُونَ ﴿٩٩﴾

None deems himself secure from Allāh's scheme save folk that perish.[172]

All of these matters should prevent the son of Ādam from resting and relaxing. A person was seen in a dream saying,

How can the eye sleep in peace and serenity?
Yet in which of the Two Abodes will it dwell?
- There is no guarantee.

One of those on his death bed, a devout worshipper, was asked about his state to which he said,

---

[171] *al-Barzakh*, refers to a barrier placed between a person who has deceased and this worldly life. It is a way of referring to the first stages of the life of the Hereafter. A very good treatment of *al-Barzakh* and the issues related to it can be found in Muhammad al-Jibaly, 'Life in *al-Barzakh*' [*Al-Kitaab & As-Sunnah* publishing, 1998].

[172] *al-A'rāf* (7): 99

None who enters the grave knows what lies awaiting
Save Allāh, the One who to the graves is leading.

In this respect one of them said,

By Allāh, were man to know for what he was created,
He would not be remiss nor would he sleep.
He was created for such a thing that be assured
Were hearts to see it neither stray would they nor sleep:
Death, then to the grave, then to be resurrected:
Rebuke dire and terrors appalling, (in this beweep!)
For the Day of Gathering have men exerted,
Praying and fasting in trepidation deep!
But we, when prohibited or commanded,
Are like the People of the Cave: awake yet asleep!

All praise is due to Allāh, Lord of the worlds.
Peace and blessings be upon our Master,
Muḥammad, his family and
all his Companions.

PICTURE PLATE OF THE MANUSCRIPT

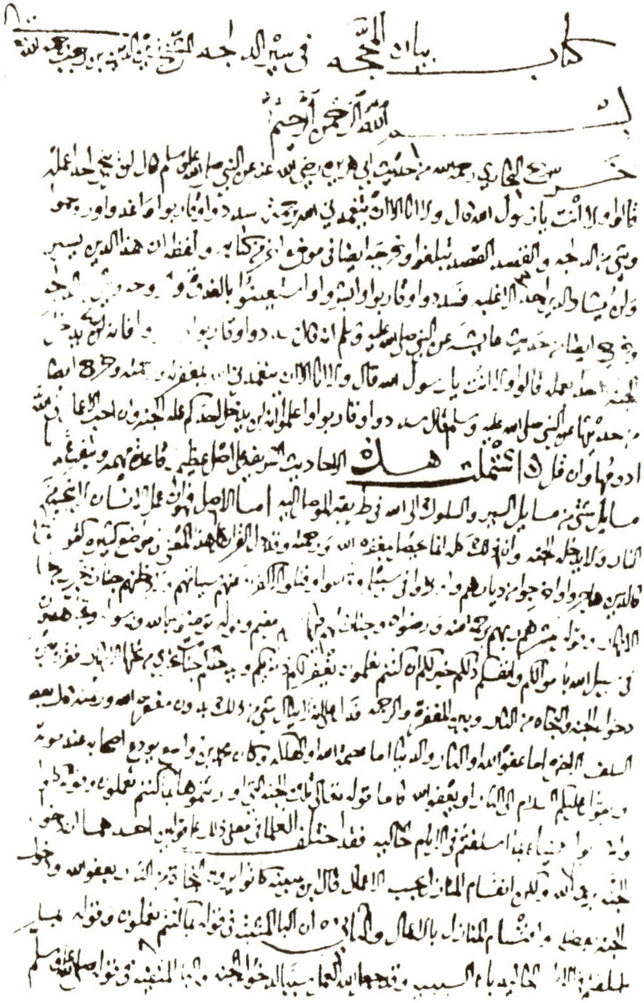

صورة الصفحة الأولى من النسخة « أ »

PICTURE PLATE OF THE MANUSCRIPT

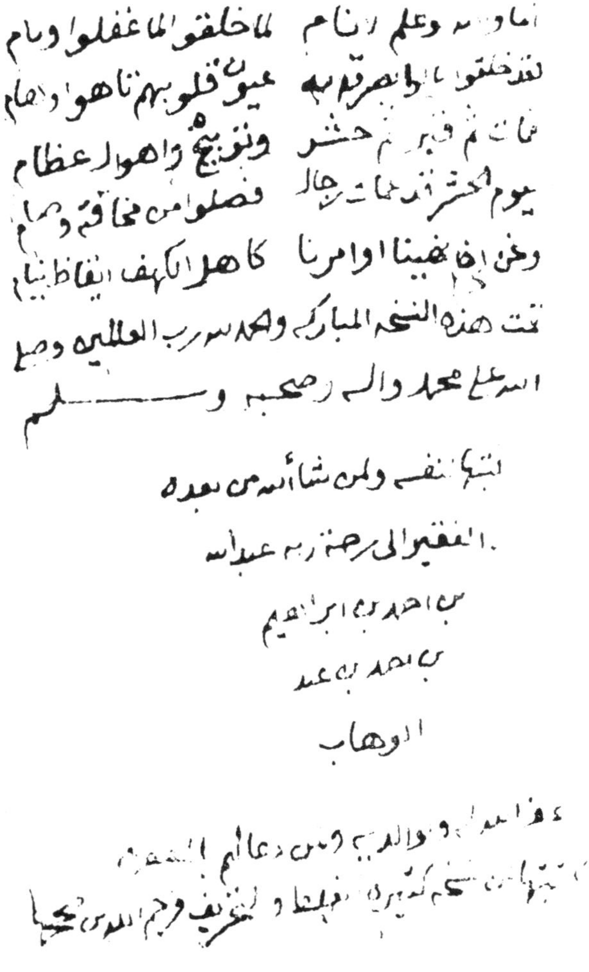

أما والله وعلم الأنام   لما خلقوا لما غفلوا وناموا

لقد خلقوا لما لو أبصرته   عيون قلوبهم تاهوا وهاموا

ممات ثم قبر ثم حشر   وتوبيخ وأهوال عظام

ليوم الحشر قد عملت رجال   فصلوا من مخافته وصاموا

ونحن إذا نهينا وأمرنا   كأهل الكهف أيقاظ نيام

تمت هذه النسخة المباركة والحمد لله رب العالمين وصلى الله على محمد وآله وصحبه وسلم

لينتفع بها نفسه ولمن شاء الله من بعده الفقير إلى رحمة ربه عبد الله بن أحمد بن إبراهيم بن أحمد بن عبد الوهاب

صورة الصفحة الأخيرة من النسخة «ب»

PICTURE PLATE OF THE MANUSCRIPT

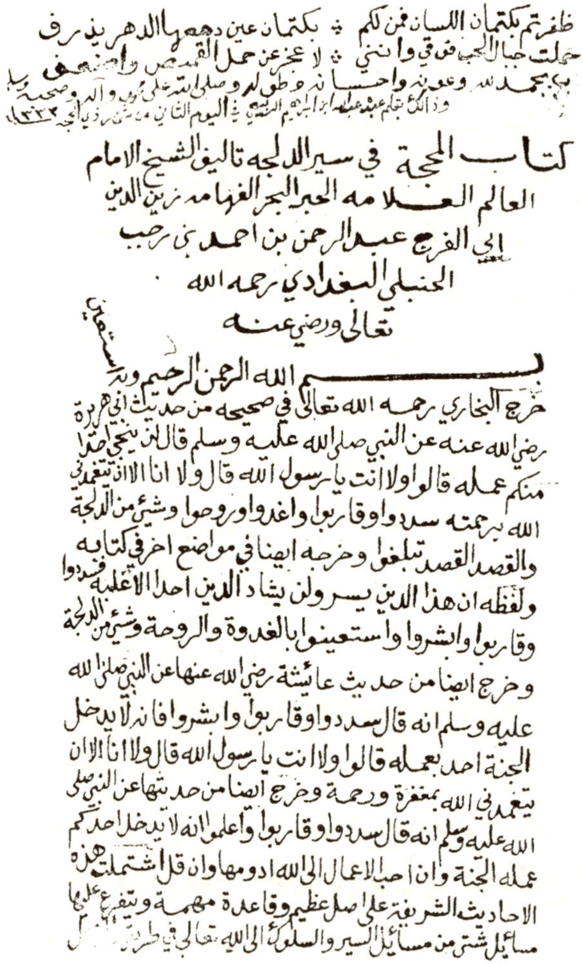
كتاب المحجة في سير الدلجة تاليف الشيخ الامام العالم العلامه الحبر البحر الفهامه زين الدين ابي الفرج عبد الرحمن بن احمد بن رجب الحنبلي البغدادي رحمه الله تعالى ورضي عنه

بسم الله الرحمن الرحيم وبه نستعين

خرج البخاري رحمه الله تعالى في صحيحه من حديث ابي هريرة رضي الله عنه عن النبي صلى الله عليه وسلم قال لن ينجي احدا منكم عمله قالوا ولا انت يا رسول الله قال ولا انا الا ان يتغمدني الله برحمته سددوا وقاربوا واغدوا وروحوا وشيء من الدلجة والقصد القصد تبلغوا وخرجه ايضا في مواضع اخر في كتابه ولفظه ان هذا الدين يسر ولن يشاد الدين احد الا غلبه فسددوا وقاربوا وابشروا واستعينوا بالغدوة والروحة وشيء من الدلجة وخرج ايضا من حديث عائشة رضي الله عنها عن النبي صلى الله عليه وسلم انه قال سددوا وقاربوا وابشروا فانه لا يدخل الجنة احد بعمله قالوا ولا انت يا رسول الله قال ولا انا الا ان يتغمدني الله بمغفرة ورحمة وخرج ايضا من حديثها عن النبي صلى الله عليه وسلم انه قال سددوا وقاربوا واعلموا انه لا يدخل احدكم عمله الجنة وان احب الاعمال الى الله ادومها وان قل اشتملت هذه الاحاديث الشريفة على اصل عظيم وقاعدة مهمة ويتفرع عليها مسائل شتى من مسائل السير والسلوك الى الله تعالى في طريق

صورة الصفحة الأولى من النسخة «ج»

PICTURE PLATE OF THE MANUSCRIPT

بسم الله الرحمن الرحيم خرج البخاري ومسلم من حديث أبي هريرة رضي الله عنه عن
النبي صلى الله عليه وسلم قال لن ينجي أحداً عمله قالوا ولا أنت يا رسول الله قال و
لا أنا إلا أن يتغمدني الله برحمة سددوا وقاربوا وروحوا واغدوا وشيء من الدلجة
والقصد القصد تبلغوا وخرجه البخاري في موضع آخر من كتابه ولفظه إن هذا الدين
يسر ولن يشاد الدين أحد إلا غلبه فسددوا وقاربوا وأبشروا واستعينوا بالغدوة
والروحة وشيء من الدلجة وخرج أيضاً من حديث عائشة عن النبي صلى الله عليه وسلم
أنه قال سددوا وقاربوا وأبشروا فإنه لا يدخل الجنة أحداً عمله قالوا ولا أنت يا رسول
الله قال ولا أنا إلا أن يتغمدني الله بمغفرة ورحمة وخرج أيضاً من حديثها عن النبي
صلى الله عليه وسلم قال سددوا وقاربوا واعلموا لن يدخل أحدكم عمله الجنة وأن أحب
الأعمال إلى الله أدومها وإن قل فقد تضمنت هذه الأحاديث الشريفة على أصل
عظيم وقاعدة مهمة ويتبع عليها سائر شيء من مسائل السير والسلوك إلى الله في
طريقه الموصل إليه أما الأصل فهو أن عمل الإنسان لا ينجيه من النار ولا يدخله الجنة
وإن ذلك كله إنما يحصل بفضل الله ورحمته وقد دل القرآن على هذا المعنى في مواضع
كثيرة كقوله تعالى فالذين هاجروا وأخرجوا من ديارهم وأوذوا في سبيلي وقاتلوا
وقتلوا لأكفرن عنهم سيئاتهم ولأدخلنهم جنات تجري من تحتها الأنهار وقوله يبشرهم
ربهم برحمة منه ورضوان وجنات لهم فيها نعيم مقيم وقوله تؤمنون بالله ورسوله وتجاهدون

صورة الصفحة الأولى من النسخة «د»

PICTURE PLATE OF THE MANUSCRIPT

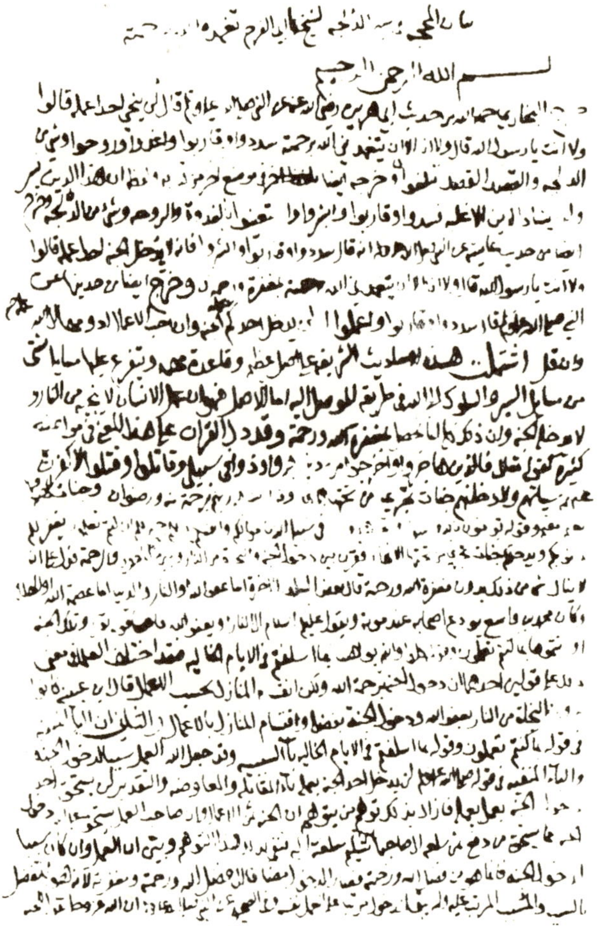
بسم الله الرحمن الرحيم

صورة الصفحة الأولى من النسخة «هـ»

Index of Arabic Words

Awliyā': plural of *walī*; friend, ally, loyal companion. From the word *wilāyah* meaning loyalty and closeness, the opposite of enmity.

'Ayy: withholding the tongue from speaking, carefully considering each word before it is said.

Barzakh: barrier, isthmus, A barrier that is erected between the deceased and this life preventing him from returning and a generic reference to the life that commences after death.

Bayān: Speech, clarification, discourse. It is of two types: the first whereby the intended meaning is expressed clearly, whatever language it may be in, this category is not regarded as magic; the second whereby the intended meaning is expressed in eloquent, cleverly doctored phrases based upon specific rules such that one listening takes pleasure in hearing the words and they affect his very heart. This category is what has been likened to magic as it captivates and beguiles the heart and overcomes the soul to the point that the face of reality could be transformed to illusion and the one captivated perceive only that which the speaker wants him to perceive. This category can be used in a commendable fashion and in a blameworthy fashion. As for the commendable form, it is to direct the person towards the truth and use these methods to aid the truth. As for the blameworthy form, it is to direct the person towards falsehood or envelop him in confusion such that the truth is seen as falsehood and falsehood as truth. This is completely blameworthy and has been likened to that which is completely blameworthy - magic

Bid'ah: innovation, that which is newly introduced into the religion of Allāh.

Ḍaʿīf: weak; the ḥadīth that is neither ṣaḥīḥ nor ḥasan because it fails to meet one of their requirements. It is of varying degrees of severity, the most severe of which being mauḍūʿ, fabricated.

Dhawq: taste, perceptivity, technically referring to spiritual experience, *dhawq* is a more temporary state of *wajd*. One may receive some forms of inspiration in the heart as a result of these states however this inspiration should always be compared to the Book and Sunnah to ascertain its correctness.

Dhikr: remembrance, recollection, technically referring the remembrance of Allāh.

Duʿā: supplication, invocation, it is an action of worship that may only be directed to Allāh. It is of two types, supplication through worship (*duʿā ʿibādah*) and supplication of request (*duʿā masʾalah*). The first type of *duʿā* can be understood when one understands that every act of worship is done with the unstated plea that Allāh accept that action of worship and the desire to draw closer to him; and hence attain His pleasure. Hence every action of worship is a type of request to Allāh. The second type of *duʿā* is whereby one explicitly asks his Lord of something such as 'O Allāh! Grant me good in this world and the Hereafter.' The second type includes the first type and the first type necessitates the second type.

Ḥadīth: A text attributed to the Prophet (ﷺ) describing his actions, words, descriptions and tacit approvals. It consists of two portions, the body of the text (*matn*) and the *isnād*. Rarely the term is also used to refer to a text attributed to a Companion or a *Tābiʿī*.

Ḥāfiẓ: pl. *Ḥuffāẓ*. Ḥadīth Master, commonly referred to one who has memorised at least 100000 ḥadīths.

Ḥasan: good, fair. A ḥadīth whose *isnād* is continuously linked of just, morally upright narrators but whose precision (*ḍabṭ*) falls short of the requirements of the ṣaḥīḥ ḥadīth; containing no irregularity (*shādh*) and no hidden defect (*ʿillah*). A ḥadīth can be ḥasan in and of itself, or contain a defect but still be ruled to be so due to supporting evidences.

Ḥayāʾ: modesty, derived from the word *ḥayāt*, or life because it is through modesty that the heart is granted life and it is through the absence of modesty that it dies. It is a state that arises through the servant being aware that Allāh is watching him, having love, fear and awe of Him and thinking little of himself. Al-Junayd said, '*al-Ḥayā'* is to recognise the bounties of Allāh and then to recognise ones own shortcomings. Through this a state is engendered which is termed *al-Ḥayā'*, the reality of which is that it is a mannerism that prevents one from committing vile actions and from being lax in fulfilling the rights of Allāh.'

Ḥudūd: limits, boundaries. The limits ordained by Allāh, prescribed punishments.

Ḥulūl wa-l-Ittiḥād: incarnation and unification, the settling of a superior faculty upon a support.

Iḥsān: beneficence, excellence. To worship Allāh as if one is seeing Him, and knowing that even though one sees Him not, He sees the servant.

Ikhlāṣ: sincerity, to strip oneself of worshiping any besides Allāh such that everything one does is performed only to draw closer to Him and for His pleasure. It is to purify ones actions from any but the Creator having a share in them, from any defect or self-desire. The one who has true *ikhlāṣ* (*mukhliṣ*) will be free of *riyā'*.

'Ilm: knowledge.

Īmān: The firm belief, complete acknowledgement and acceptance of all that Allāh and His Messenger have commanded to have faith in, submitting to it both inwardly and outwardly. It is the acceptance and belief of the heart that includes the actions of the heart and body, therefore it encompasses the establishment of the whole religion. This is why the Imāms and Salaf used to say, 'Faith is the statement of the heart and tongue, action of the heart, tongue and limbs.' Hence it comprises statement, action and belief, it increases through obedience and decreases through disobedience. It includes the beliefs of faith, its morals and manners and the actions demanded by it.

Islām: submission, submitting to the will of Allāh through following His law as revealed upon the tongue of the Messenger (ﷺ).

Isnād: support. The chain of authorities on which a narration is based, linking the end narrator of a narration to the one it is attributed to, be it the Prophet (ﷺ) or anyone else, narrator by narrator.

Istidrāj: gradually leading to a desired conclusion. Technically refers to Allāh gradually leading one who displays ingratitude to His favours to his destruction as a befitting recompense. Some of the Salaf would say, 'When you see Allāh bestowing His blessings upon you, one after the other, and you are steadfast in disobeying Him, then beware for this is *istidrāj* by which He gradually leads you to destruction.'

Ittibā': following, technically referring to following the Sunnah of the Prophet (ﷺ).

'Iyāfah: the practice of divination through frightening birds, the sounds they make and the directions in which they fly.

Jāhiliyyah: Pre-Islāmic Ignorance. Technically this refers to the condition of a people before the guidance of Allāh reaches them, or the state of a people that prevents them from accepting the guidance of Allāh.

Jahl: ignorance.

Kalām: speech, discourse. Technically used to refer to dialectics and scholastic theology.

Khalaf: successors. A reference to those who followed a path other than the path of the Salaf.

Khalīfah: pl. *khulafā'*. Successor, representative. The Successors of the Prophet (ﷺ), head of the Islāmic state. Also called *Amīr al-Mu'minīn* or Leader of the Believers.

Khushū': submissiveness, humility.

Kufr: denial, rejection, hiding, technically referring to disbelief. It can be major (removing a person from the fold of Islām) or minor (not removing a person from the fold of Islām).

Majhūl: unknown. A reference to a narrator from whom only one narrator narrates (*majhūl al-'ain*) or whose state of precision (*ḍabṭ*) is unknown (*majhūl al-ḥāl*), such a narrator makes the *isnād ḍa'īf*.

Ma'rifah: gnosis. Knowledge that is acted upon by the one who knows, the Gnostic of Allāh is one who has knowledge of Allāh, the path that leads to Allāh and the pitfalls of that path. He is one who knows Allāh, His Names, Attributes and Actions and then displays *ṣidq* and *ikhlāṣ* towards Allāh in all things. He works towards removing all despicable morals and mannerisms and has *ṣabr* in all of this.

Matrūk: abandoned. A narrator who is accused of lying, or makes many mistakes, or makes mistakes in aḥādith that are agreed upon, or narrates from famous narrators that which those narrators do not know.

Mudallis: one who does *tadlīs*

Munqaṭi': that ḥadīth from which the narrator just before the Companion has been omitted from its *isnād*.

Murāqabah: self-inspection. The servant having the sure knowledge that Allāh sees him in all circumstances and knows all that he is doing, as such the he does his utmost not to fall into the prohibited matters and to correct his own failings.

Mursal: disconnected. A ḥadīth whereby a *Tābi'ī* narrates directly from the Prophet (ﷺ) without mentioning the Companion. In the view of the majority of Scholars it is a sub-category of ḍa'īf.

Qadr: Divine Decree and Destiny.

Qur'ān: The actual Word of Allāh revealed to the Prophet (ﷺ) in the Arabic language through the medium of the Angel Gabriel and the greatest miracle bestowed him. It consists of 114 chapters commencing with al-Fātiḥah and ending with an-Nās.

Riyā': showing off, ostentation, an example of which lies in person beautifying actions of worship because he knows people are watching.

Ruqyā: recitation used to cure an illness or disease. It can only be done in the Arabic tongue, in words whose meaning is understood, using verses of the Qur'ān or supplications of the Prophet combined with the belief that it is only Allāh who in reality gives the cure.

Ṣabr: patience and steadfastness, the restraint of ones self to that which is dictated by the divine law. It is of three levels, steadfastness in the obedience of Allāh, steadfastness in avoiding the prohibited matters and patience at the onset of calamity. *Ikhlāṣ* can never be complete without *ṣidq* and *ṣidq* can never be complete without *ikhlāṣ* and the two can never be complete without *ṣabr*. The person is patient through Allāh, i.e. seeking His aid Alone; for Allāh, i.e. arising out of love for Him and the desire to draw close to Him; and with Allāh, i.e. doing only that which He wills.

Ṣaḥābah: The Companions of the Prophet (ﷺ), those who saw him, believed in him and died upon that belief.

Ṣāḥīḥ: correct, authentic. A ḥadith which has a continuously linked *isnād*, of just, morally upright and precise narrators; containing no irregularity (*shādh*) or hidden defect (*'illah*). Hence five conditions have to be met: the *isnād* being continuously linked; the justice (*'adl*) of the narrator; the precision (*ḍabṭ*) of the narrator; its not being *shādh*; and its not containing an *'illah*. The ḥadīth can be ṣaḥīḥ in and of itself, or it can contain a defect but still be ruled to be ṣaḥīḥ due to supporting evidences.

Salaf: predecessors. Technically used to refer to the best generations of Muslims, the first three generation: the *Ṣaḥābah*, the *Tābi'ūn* and the *Tab' Tābi'ūn* due to the ḥadīth, 'The best of people are my generation, then the one that follows, then the one that follows.'

Ṣidq: truthfulness, the conformity of the inner to the outer such that the deeds and statements of the person do not belie his beliefs and vice-versa. *Ṣidq* is the foundation of faith and results in peace of mind, lying is the foundation of hypocrisy and results in doubt and suspicion, and this is why the two can never co-exist without being at odds with each other. al-Junayd was asked as to whether *ṣidq* and *ikhlāṣ* were the same or different and he replied, 'They are different, *ṣidq* is the root and *ikhlāṣ* is the branch. *Ṣidq* is the foundation of everything and *ikhlāṣ* only comes into play once one commences an action. Actions are only acceptable when they combine both.' The one who has true *ṣidq* will be free of self-conceit.

Shādh: irregular, odd. A ḥadīth narrated by a trustworthy and precise narrator that contradicts the narrative of other narrators or the narration of one more trustworthy and precise than him, provided that a reconciliation is not possible.

Shirk: association, technically referring to directing a right that is due to Allāh Alone to another object of creation, either completely or partially. It can be major (removing a person from the fold of Islām) or minor (not removing a person from the fold of Islām).

Sunnah: way, path. The actions, words, descriptions, commands, prohibitions and tacit approvals of the Prophet (ﷺ).

Tābi'ūn: The generation following that of the Companions.

Tab' Tābi'ūn: The generation following that of the *Tābi'ūn*.

Tadlīs: deceit. An action of a narrator whereby he makes out that he heard something from a particular narrator what he did not hear or conceals the identity of the one he is narrating from. In order to do so, he will use terms that are vague such as 'such-and-such said' and 'on the authority of such-and-such.' The first type of *tadlīs* is blameworthy and constitutes a defect in the *isnād*. The second is dependant upon exactly what was done and the motives of the narrator, it can be blameworthy or not.

Taqwā: the basic meaning of which is setting a barrier between two things. This is why it is said that one *ittaqā* with his shield, i.e. he set it as a barrier between him and the one who wished him evil. Therefore it is as if the one who has taqwa (*muttaqī*) has used his following the commands of Allāh and avoiding His prohibitions as a barrier between himself and the Punishment. Hence he has preserved and fortified himself against the punishment of Allāh through his obeying Him.

Ṭarq: the practice of divination through drawing lines in the earth or equally the practice of throwing gravel onto the ground and divination by the shapes subsequently formed therein.

Tawḥīḍ: unification, monotheism, the belief in the absolute Oneness of Allāh. It is to believe that Allāh Alone is the creator, nourisher, and sustainer of the worlds; it is to believe that Allāh Alone deserves to be worshipped; and it is to believe that He has unique and perfect Names and Attributes that far transcend anything that one can imagine.

Ṭiyarah: seeing bad omens in things.

Waḥdatu-l-Wujūd: The unity of existence, the heretical belief that Allāh is everywhere and everything.

Wajd: strong emotion, technically referring to spiritual ecstasy. The heart experiencing sudden surges of intense love, desire, awe and glorification of Allāh.

Wara': pious caution, scrupulousness. A mannerism through which the heart is purified of all that would sully it and has been excellently summarised in the saying of the Prophet (ﷺ), "From the excellence of ones Islām is his leaving that which does not concern him." It is to leave all that causes one doubt, all that does not concern him, to continuously bring oneself to account and to devote oneself to Allāh. Some of the Salaf said, 'None attains the reality of *taqwā* until he leaves that which is harmless for fear of falling into that which is harmful.'

Yaqīn: certainty. It is to faith (*Īmān*) what the soul is to the body, it is the soul to the actions of the heart which in turn formulate the souls to the actions of the limbs and through it one attains the rank of Ṣiddīq. From *yaqīn* does *tawakkul* (absolute reliance in Allāh) sprout and through *yaqīn* is all doubt, suspicion and worry dispelled and the heart filled with love, hope and fear of Allāh. *Yaqīn* is of three levels, that which arises from knowledge (*'ilm al-yaqīn*), seeing (*'ain al-yaqīn*) and actual experience (*Ḥaqq al-yaqīn*).

Translators Bibliography

al-Ājurrī, Abū Bakr Muḥammad ibn al-Ḥusayn

ash-Sharī'ah [Dār al-Waṭan, Riyadh, 1st ed. 1997/1418, notes by 'Abdullāh ibn Sulaymān, 5+1 vols]

Ṣifātu-l-Ghurabā' [Dār al-Khulafā' li-l-Kitāb al-Islāmī, 2nd ed., with the notes of Badr ibn 'Abdullāh al-Badr]

al-Albānī, Muḥammad Nāṣir ad-Dīn,

Ḍa'īf Abū Dāwūd [al-Maktab al-Islāmī, Beirūt, 1st ed. 1991/1412]

Ḍa'īf ibn Mājah [al-Maktab al-Islāmī, Beirūt, 1st ed. 1988/1408]

Ḍa'īf al-Jāmi' as-Ṣaghīr [al-Maktab al-Islāmī, Beir˘t, 3rd ed. 1990/1410]

Ḍa'īf at-Targhīb wa-t-Tarhīb [Maktabah al-Ma'ārif, Riyādh, 1st ed. 2000/1421, 2 vols]

'ilāl al-Jannah [al-Maktab al-Islāmī, Beirūt, 2nd ed. 1985/1405]

Ghāyatu-l-Marām [al-Maktab al-Islāmī, Beirūt, 4th ed. 1994/1414]

Irwā' al-Ghalīl [al-Maktab al-Islāmī, Beirūt, 2nd ed. 1985/1405, 8+1 vols.]

Ṣaḥīḥ Abū Dāwūd [al-Maktab al-Islāmī, Beirūt, 1st ed. 1989/1409, 3 vols.]

Ṣaḥīḥ Adab al-Mufrad [Dār as-Ṣiddīq, al-Jubayl, 2nd ed. 1994/1415]

Ṣaḥīḥ ibn Mājah [al-Maktab al-Islāmī, Beirūt, 1st ed. 1986/

1407, 2 vols.]

Ṣaḥīḥ al-Jāmi' as-Ṣaghīr [al-Maktab al-Islāmī, Beirūt, 3rd ed. 1988/1408, 2 vols.]

Ṣaḥīḥ at-Tirmidhī [al-Maktab al-Islāmī, Beirūt, 1st ed. 1988/1408, 3 vols.]

Ṣaḥīḥ at-Targhīb wa-t-Tarhīb [Maktabah al-Ma'ārif, Riyādh, 1st ed. 2000/1421, 3 vols.]

Silsilah Aḥādīth as-Ṣaḥīḥah [Maktabah al-Ma'ārif, Riyādh, 2nd ed. 1986/1407, 10 vols.]

Silsilah Aḥādith ad-Ḍa'īfah [Maktabah al-Ma'ārif, Riyādh, 5th ed. 1992/1412, 12 vols.]

Tamām al-Minnah [Dār ar-Rāyah, Riyādh, 3rd ed. 1989/1409]

Abu Nu'aym, Aḥmad ibn 'Abdullāh al-Aṣfahānī

Ḥilyatu-l-Awliyā' [Dār al-Kutub al-'Ilmiyyah, Beirut, 1st ed. 1997/1418, notes by Mutṣaphā 'Aṭā', 12+2 vols.]

al-'Adhīm'Abādī, Abū at-Ṭayyib Muḥammad Shamsu-l-Ḥaqq

'Awn al-Ma'būd Sharḥ Sunan Abū Dawūd [al-Maktabah as-Salafiyyah, Medina, 2nd ed. 1969/1388, in the margin of which is ibn al-Qayyim, *Sharḥ Abū Dāwūd*, 13 vols.]

Aḥmad ibn Ḥanbal

Musnad [Mu'assasah ar-Risālah, Beirut, 1st ed. 1995/1416, notes by Shu'ayb al-Arna'ūṭ et. al., 45+5 vols.]

al-Baghawī, Abū Muḥammad al-Ḥusayn ibn Mas'ūd al-Farā'

Sharḥ as-Sunnah [al-Maktab al-Islāmī, Beir˘t, 2nd ed. 1983/1403, notes by Shu'ayb al-Arna'ūṭ, 15+1 vols.]

al-Bayhaqī, Abū Bakr Aḥmad ibn al-Ḥusayn

Shu'ab al-īmān [Dār al-Kutub al-'Ilmiyyah, Beirut, 1st ed. 1990/1410, notes by Muḥammad Zaghlūl, 7+2 vols.]

Dalā'il an-Nubuwwah [Dār al-Kutub al-'Ilmiyyah, Beirut, 1st ed. 1985/1405, ed. A. Qal'ajī, 6+1 vols.]

Sunan al-Kubrā [Dār al-Fikr, 1st ed. 1996/1416, 15 vols.]

adh-Dhahabī, Muḥammad ibn Aḥmad,

Siyar al-A'lām an-Nubulā' [Mu'assasah Risālah, 11th ed. 1996/1417, ed. S. al-Arna'ūt, 23+2 vols.]

Tartīb al-Mawḍū'āt [Dār al-Kutub al-'Ilmiyyah, Beirut, 1st Ed. 1994/1415]

al-Ghazālī, Abū Ḥāmid

Iḥyā' 'Ulūm ad-Dīn [Dār al-Khayr, 4th Ed. 1997/1417, notes by al-'Irāqī, 5 vols.]

al-Ḥākim, Muḥammad ibn 'Abdullāh,

al-Mustadrak 'alā as-Ṣaḥīḥayn [Dār al-Kutub al-'Ilmiyyah, Beirut, 4+1 vols.]

Ibn 'Abdu-l-Barr, Abū 'Umar Yūsuf

Jāmi' al-Bayān al-'Ilm [Dār ibn al-Jawzī, Dammām, 4th ed. 1998/1419, notes by Abū al-Ashbāl az-Zuhayrī, 2 vols]

Tamhīd, [Dār Kutub 'Ilmiyyah, Beirut, 1999/1419, 10+1 vols.]

Ibn Ḥajr, Shihābu-d-Dīn Aḥmad ibn 'Alī ibn Muḥammad

Fatḥ al-Bārī [Dār al-Kutub al-'Ilmiyyah, Beirut, 1st ed. 1989/1410, notes by 'Abdu-l-'Azīz ibn Bāz, 13+2 vols.]

Maṭālib al-'Āliyah [Dār al-Waṭan, Riyādh, 1st ed. 1997/1418, notes by Ghunaym ibn Ghunaym, 4+1 vols.]

Talkhīṣ al-Ḥabīr [Mu'assasah Qurṣuba, 1st ed. 1995/1416, 4 vols.]

Ibn Ḥibbān, Abū Ḥātim Muḥammad

Rawḍatu-l-'Uqalā [Dār ash-Sharīf, Riyādh, 2nd ed. 1997/1418, notes by Ibrāhīm al-Ḥāzimī]

Ṣaḥīḥ, [Mu'assasatu-l-Risālah, 2nd ed. 1997/1418, notes by Shu'ayb al-Arna'ūṭ, 16+2 vols.]

Ibn al-Jawzī, Abū-l-Farah 'Abdur-Raḥmān,

al-Mawḍū'āt [Dār al-Fikr, 2nd ed. 1983/1403, 3 vols.]

Ibn Kathīr, Abū al-Fiḍā' Ismā'īl,

al-Bidāyah wa-n-Nihāyah [Dār Iḥyā at-Turāth al-'Arabī, Beirut, 1993/1413, 14+1 vols.]

Ibn al-Qayyim, Shamsu-d-Dīn Abu ʿAbdullāh Muḥammad

al-Fawāʾid [Dār al-Kitāb al-ʿArabī, Beirut, 5th Ed 1993/1414, notes by Muḥammad ʿUthmān]

Madārij as-Sālikīn [Dār al-Kitāb al-ʿArabī, Beirut, 3 vols.]

Ibn Qutaybah,

Taʾwīl Mukhtalif al-Aḥādīth [Dār al-Kitāb al-ʿArabī, Beirut]

Ibn Rajab, ʿAbdur-Raḥmān ibn Aḥmad Zaynu-d-Dīn

Faḍl ʿIlm as-Salaf ʿalā al-Khalaf [Dār ʿAmmār, Ammān, 1st ed. 1986/1406, notes by ʿAlī Ḥasan]

Faḍl ʿIlm as-Salaf ʿalā al-Khalaf [Dār al-Arqam, Kuwait, 1st ed. 1983/1404, notes by Aḥmad an-Najmī]

Fatḥ al-Bārī Sharḥ Ṣaḥīḥ al-Bukhārī [Dār ibn al-Jawzī, 2nd ed. 1422, ed. Ṭ. ʿIwaḍullāh, 7 vols.]

al-Ḥākim, Abū ʿAbdullāh Muḥammad ibn ʿAbdullāh

al-Mustadrak ʿalā as-Ṣaḥīḥayn [Dār al-Kutub al-ʿIlmiyyah, Beirut, 1st ed.1990/1411, notes by Muṣṭapha ʿAṭāʾ, 4+1 vols.]

al-Haythamī, Nūru-d-Dīn ʿAlī ibn Abū Bakr

Majmaʿ az-Zawāʾid [Dār al-Kutub al-ʿIlmiyyah, Beirut]

al-ʿIjlūnī, Ismāʿīl ibn Muḥammad,

Kashf al-Khafāʾ [Dār al-Kutub al-ʿIlmiyyah, Beirut, 3rd ed. 1988/1408]

al-ʿIrāqī, Abū al-Faḍl Zayn ad-Dīn ʿAbdur-Raḥīm,

al-Mughnī ʿan Ḥamal al-Asfār [Dār at-Ṭabariyyah, 1st ed 1995/1415, notes Ashraf ʿAbdu-l-Maqṣūd, 2+1 vols.]

al-Mubārakpūrī, Abū-l-ʿAlā Muḥammad ʿAbdur-Raḥmān,

Tuḥfatu-l-Aḥwadhī Sharḥ Sunan at-Tirmidhī [Dār al-Kutub al-ʿIlmiyyah, Beirut, 1st ed. 1990/1410, 10 vols.]

al-Munāwī, Muḥammad ʿAbdur-Raʾūf

Fayḍ al-Qadīr [Dār al-Kutub al-ʿIlmiyyah, Beirut, 1st ed. 1994/1415, notes by Aḥmad ʿAbdus-Salām, 6 vols.]

an-Nawawī, Yaḥyā ibn Sharaf,

Sharḥ Ṣaḥīḥ Muslim [Dār al-Kutub al-ʿIlmiyyah, Beirut, 1st ed. 1995/1415, 18+1 vols.]

as-Sakhāwī, Muḥammad 'Abdur-Raḥmān,

Maqāṣid al-Ḥasanah [Dār al-Kitāb al-'Arabī, Beirut, 2nd ed. 1994/1414, ed. M. 'Uthmān]

as-Suyūṭī, Jalālu-d-Dīn 'Abdur-Raḥmān ibn Abū Bakr

ad-Durr al-Manthūr [Dār al-Kutub al-'Ilmiyyah, Beirut, 1st ed. 2000/1421, 6+1 vols.]

al-Lalī' al-Maṣnū'ah [Dār al-Kutub al-'Ilmiyyah, Beirut, 1st ed. 1996/1417, 2+1 vols.]

at-Ṭāḥāwī, Abū Ja'far Aḥmad ibn Muḥammad,

Sharḥ Mushkil al-Āthār [Mu'assasah ar-Risālah, Beirut, 1st ed. 1994/1415, ed. Shu'ayb al-Arna'ūṭ, 15+1 vols.]

az-Zurqānī, Muḥammad ibn 'Abdul-Bāqī,

Sharḥ Muwaṭṭa Mālik [Dār al-Kutub al-'Ilmiyyah, Beirut, 4 vols.]

DĀR AS-SUNNAH PUBLISHERS

IBN RAJAB SERIES

The EXCELLENCE of KNOWLEDGE
of the *Salaf* over that of the *Khalaf*
being a translation of his *Faḍl 'Ilm al-Salaf 'alā'l-Khalaf*
ISBN 1-904336-19-1

HUMILITY in PRAYER
being a translation of his
al-Khushū' fi'l-Ṣalāh or *al-Dhull wa'l-Inkisār li'l-'Azīz al-Jabbār*
ISBN 1-904336-21-3

The JOURNEY to ALLĀH
An explanation to the Ḥadīth,
"Your actions alone will not save any of you"
being a translation of his *al-Maḥajjah fi Sayri'l-Dulja*
ISBN 1-904336-17-5

The KEY to PARADISE
An explanation to the Testimony of Faith
and its Benefits
being a translation of his *Taḥqīq Kalimatu'l-Ikhlāṣ*
ISBN 1-904336-20-5

The LEGACY of the PROPHET
An explanation to the Advice given to ibn 'Abbās,
being a translation of his
Nūr al-Iqtibās fī Sharḥ Waṣiyyah al-Nabī li ibn 'Abbās
ISBN 1-904336-22-1

The HEAVENLY DISPUTE
being a translation of his
Ikhtiyār al-Awlā Sharḥ Ikhtiṣām al-Mala' al-A'lā
ISBN 1-904336-33-X

The JOURNEY of the STRANGERS
being a translation of his *Kashfu'l-Kurbah fī Wasfi Ḥāli Ahli-l-Ghurbah*, also a translation of *Ṣifatu-l-Ghurabā'* of
Imām Abū Bakr al-Ājurrī
ISBN 1-904336-18-3